Spoken Dialogue Systems

Synthesis Lectures on Human Language Technologies

Editor

Graeme Hirst, University of Toronto

Synthesis Lectures on Human Language Technologies publishes monographs on topics relating to natural language processing, computational linguistics, information retrieval, and spoken language understanding. Emphasis is placed on important new techniques, on new applications, and on topics that combine two or more HLT subfields.

Spoken Dialogue Systems
Kristiina Jokinen, Michael McTear
2010

Introduction to Chinese Natural Language Processing
Kam-Fai Wong, Wenji Li, Ruifeng Xu, Zheng-sheng Zhang
2009

Introduction to Linguistic Annotation and Text Analytics
Graham Wilcock
2009

Dependency Parsing
Sandra Kübler, Ryan McDonald, Joakim Nivre
2009

Statistical Language Models for Information Retrieval
ChengXiang Zhai
2008

Spoken Dialogue Systems
Kristiina Jokinen and Michael McTear
www.morganclaypool.com

ISBN: 9781598295993 paperback

ISBN: 9781598296006 ebook

DOI: 10.2200/S00204ED1V01Y200910HLT005

A Publication in the Morgan & Claypool Publishers series

SYNTHESIS LECTURES ON HUMAN LANGUAGE TECHNOLOGIES

Lecture #5

Series Editor: Graeme Hirst, University of Toronto

Series ISSN

ISSN   1947-4040   print
ISSN   1947-4059   electronic

Spoken Dialogue Systems

Kristiina Jokinen
University of Helsinki

Michael McTear
University of Ulster

SYNTHESIS LECTURES ON HUMAN LANGUAGE TECHNOLOGIES #5

MORGAN & CLAYPOOL PUBLISHERS

ABSTRACT

Considerable progress has been made in recent years in the development of dialogue systems that support robust and efficient human–machine interaction using spoken language. Spoken dialogue technology allows various interactive applications to be built and used for practical purposes, and research focuses on issues that aim to increase the system's communicative competence by including aspects of error correction, cooperation, multimodality, and adaptation in context.

This book gives a comprehensive view of state-of-the-art techniques that are used to build spoken dialogue systems. It provides an overview of the basic issues such as system architectures, various dialogue management methods, system evaluation, and also surveys advanced topics concerning extensions of the basic model to more conversational setups.

The goal of the book is to provide an introduction to the methods, problems, and solutions that are used in dialogue system development and evaluation. It presents dialogue modelling and system development issues relevant in both academic and industrial environments and also discusses requirements and challenges for advanced interaction management and future research.

KEYWORDS

Spoken dialogue systems, multimodality, evaluation, error-handling, dialogue management, statistical method

Contents

Preface

A spoken dialogue system enables a human user to access information and services that are available on a computer or over the Internet using spoken language as the medium of interaction. In future visions of interaction technology, the talking computer is portrayed as all-knowing, highly articulate, and often humanlike, with the ability to provide all types of useful information, react to a wide range of situations and problems, and recognize gestures and emotions. However, the reality of current spoken dialogue systems falls well short of their counterparts in science fiction. Commercially available systems are able to automate a variety of customer services, such as providing flight information, weather forecasts, sports results, and share prices, and they can also support transactions such as booking hotels, renting cars, making payments, or downloading ring tones for mobile phones. These systems free human operators from mundane tasks that are repetitive in nature and can thus be easily automated, and for which a spoken dialogue is also a natural mode of communication. However, research laboratories across the world are continually pushing back the frontiers by developing systems with more advanced capabilities. These systems have a more conversational interface and they deal with more difficult tasks such as planning the evacuation of a disaster area or troubleshooting a faulty piece of equipment for a customer. Other research is concerned with making systems more attentive to human needs as well as showing humanlike characteristics in their responses, for example, by enabling the systems to recognize the emotional states of their users and by similarly displaying appropriate emotions in the course of a dialogue.

Spoken dialogue systems differ from other applications that use speech for input and/or output, such as dictation systems, command-and-control systems, and text-to-speech systems. Dictation systems use speech recognition to transcribe a user's speech into words and sentences, but do not process the transcribed data any further, whereas command-and-control systems interpret user commands, such as "Make this bold" or "Switch on the light," by translating the words into a system action. Similarly, text-to-speech systems, such as screen readers or SMS readers for mobile phones, produce spoken output from a segment of written text but do not otherwise engage the user in any interaction.

Spoken dialogue systems, on the other hand, although incorporating the core technologies of automatic speech recognition and text-to-speech synthesis, also require ways of maintaining a dialogue with the user. This can involve making decisions about how to interpret the user's input and what action to take next—for example, whether to confirm that the user's input has been correctly understood, to ask a follow-up question, to check information in a database, and so on. These decisions are the responsibility of the Dialogue Manager, which is the central, controlling component of a spoken dialogue system. On one hand, dialogue management can be implemented using techniques that aim at efficient and robust performance in fairly simple interactive applications. On the other hand, dialogue management can also aim to approximate a conversational style of interaction that requires more complex models and techniques, and for which ongoing research and experimentation have proposed a number of different solutions. In general, this subarea of spoken language technology is referred to as Spoken Dialogue Technology (McTear, 2004).

This book provides an overview of the basic issues concerning the design and development of spoken dialogue systems. It covers the history and breadth of various approaches in the research community, and also introduces new approaches and issues that are the topics of current research. It also integrates academic research with approaches common in industry, and discusses recent advances in the light of what dialogue systems are trying to accomplish and how to evaluate their performance.

The book is meant for students and teachers alike, as a first textbook on the main topics in spoken dialogue technology. It aims at providing comprehensible definitions of the various concepts and issues, as well as of detailed descriptions of implemented systems, and it thus also functions as a handbook on spoken dialogue technology. It can be read by students with either engineering or humanities backgrounds.

The structure of the book is as follows. Chapter 1 provides an introduction to spoken dialogue systems, beginning with two examples, one of a commercial system and one of a research system, that illustrate some of the capabilities of current spoken dialogue systems. The examples are followed by a presentation of a typical spoken dialogue system architecture and description of the main processes that take place from the interpretation of the user's spoken input to the production of the system's response. The functions of the main system components that support these processes—speech recognition, spoken language understanding, dialogue management, response generation, and text to speech synthesis—are discussed and the main methods for performing these functions are reviewed. An overview of typical application domains is also presented. This is followed by a discussion about the collection and management of dialogue corpora to support the development and evaluation processes, and by an introduction to the issue of evaluation. Finally, the chapter presents some toolkits and software products that can be used to develop and run spoken dialogue applications.

Chapter 2 looks at dialogue management in more detail in terms of the two main tasks: dialogue control and dialogue context modeling. Dialogue control is concerned with controlling the flow of the dialogue, whereas dialogue context modeling deals with the maintenance of a representation of contextual information relevant to the dialogue, and is used by the dialogue manager to interpret the user's input and inform the user of the decisions of dialogue control. A number of the most common methods and techniques for implementing dialogue control, including graph-based and frame-based approaches, are illustrated along with a discussion of their strengths and weaknesses. This is followed by an overview of VoiceXML a standard developed within the World Wide Web Consortium for specifying dialogues that is used widely in commercial systems. The second part of the chapter examines issues concerned with dialogue context modeling, in particular methods for keeping track of the current state of the dialogue and for representing those aspects of the context that are relevant to dialogue management. The chapter concludes with an overview of the statistical and machine learning approaches to dialogue management. Although traditionally, most work on dialogue management has specified and implemented rules that determine dialogue control and context updates in an algorithmic manner, recent research has explored an alternative approach in which dialogue management is learned automatically from data, and no explicit rules are used to represent the relations between input and output, or how the context is maintained.

The potential for error is an important consideration for developers of spoken dialogue applications as well as for those who aim to deploy the applications in real-world environments. This is particularly important given the impact of errors on system performance and user satisfaction. Chapter 3 provides an overview of different approaches to error handling for spoken dialogue systems, looking at methods for error detection, error prediction, and recovery from error. Earlier methods for handling errors are rule-based, but more recently researchers have been exploring a range of data-driven approaches within a statistical framework. The second part of the chapter reviews this work, looking at how decisions regarding whether and how to handle errors are based on such criteria as the costs and benefits of using a particular strategy.

Chapter 4 presents a number of case studies that represent the current state of the art in dialogue management research. Although the basics of dialogue management, including standard methods for dialogue control and dialogue context modeling were reviewed in Chapter 2, the systems discussed in Chapter 4 extend the introduced dialogue control strategies and models in various ways. The first section presents Information State Theory, which provides a theoretically grounded method for representing dialogue context as well as a flexible mechanism for dialogue control using update rules. This is followed by an overview of the Rochester TRIPS system as an example of the plan-based approach to dialogue management that originated in artificial intelligence research in 1990s. A third trend in dialogue research is to develop architectures based on software agents that perform specific functions within the overall system. The Queen's Communicator illustrates an object-oriented approach to software agents, where more specific agents can inherit properties and behaviors of more generic agents. A different use of software agents is illustrated in the AthosMail system, where multiple agents are used to deal with small dialogue tasks in different ways, such as how to generate different types of confirmation or take different types of dialogue initiative. In the final section, two case studies are presented of systems that make use of statistical methods—the Conversational Architectures Project, which presents a computational model of grounding and a treatment of dialogue as a process of decision making under uncertainty, and the DIHANA system, which illustrates corpus-based dialogue management.

Chapter 5 is concerned with the question of how to make interaction with automated spoken dialogue systems more natural by examining the properties and processes of dialogues between humans. A range of different issues are discussed and illustrated, using examples from recent dialogue research, including: cooperation, communicative competence, adaptation, multimodality, and natural interaction—that is, the extent to which interaction with a dialogue system can be natural, enjoyable and satisfying for a user.

Evaluation plays an important role in the dialogue systems development process, both in terms of objective criteria that measure the performance of a system as well as subjective criteria that reflect the judgments of users of the system. A brief introduction to evaluation was presented in Chapter 1. Chapter 6 examines evaluation in greater detail, looking at a variety of different measures and metrics that have been used as well as the goals that these methods address. Detailed illustrations of a range of evaluation frameworks are provided. The chapter concludes with an overview of recent work on automation in evaluation and discusses the issues involved in the evaluation of advanced dialogue systems exhibiting the features of more intelligent conversational interaction described in Chapter 5.

Chapter 7 briefly summarizes the main contents of the book and explores future directions. Although the book has focused on task-based systems in which dialogue is used to perform a task, such as booking a flight or making a hotel reservation, there has also been another line of research on systems that simulate conversation. A brief overview is provided of work in this area. After this, the final section examines the relationship between academic and commercial research and development, indicating some of the differences in aims and methods, but also pointing to how the academic and commercial communities might work more closely together.

C H A P T E R 1

Introduction to Spoken Dialogue Systems

There are two main types of spoken dialogue systems: task-oriented and nontask-oriented. Task-oriented systems involve the use of dialogues to accomplish a task, which may be a fairly simple and well-defined task such as making a hotel booking, or a more complex task involving planning and reasoning, such as planning a family holiday, negotiating a contract, or managing a disaster scenario. Nontask-oriented systems, on the other hand, engage in conversational interaction, but without necessarily being involved in a task that needs to be accomplished. Naturally, there may be some overlap between the two types of system, for example, in task-oriented systems the participants might also engage in conversational interaction, and in nontask-oriented systems they may also be involved in solving a task. It should also be noted that the term conversational is often used in the literature to describe task-oriented systems that use more complex spoken language and dialogue styles than the more restricted system-initiative systems in which the system controls the interaction and the user's input is confined to short and predictable responses.

In this chapter, we introduce the main topics and issues related to spoken dialogue system design and development. First, in Section 1.1, two examples of spoken dialogue systems are presented: (1) a commercial system developed at AT&T for call routing and (2) a research system developed at the Massachusetts Institute of Technology (MIT) for providing travel information. Several differences between the two systems are noted and discussed. Following this, a basic architecture for spoken dialogue systems is introduced in Section 1.2, and the main processes that take place during a cycle through the components of this architecture are described. Section 1.3 gives an overview of some typical applications of spoken dialogue technology, while in Section 1.4 the issues of data collection and the use of dialogue corpora are discussed. Section 1.5 introduces the topic of dialogue system evaluation, which is discussed in greater detail in Chapter 6. Finally, in Section 1.6, several toolkits and software products are introduced that can be used to develop and run spoken dialogue applications.

1.1   EXAMPLES OF SPOKEN DIALOGUE SYSTEMS

One of the earliest spoken dialogue systems to be deployed commercially is the AT&T How May I Help You? (HMIHY) system, which handles about 15 million calls per month (Gorin et al., 1997; Gupta et al., 2006). HMIHY is a call routing system that classifies customer calls and routes them to the correct destination. The following is an example of a successful interaction with the system (Walker et al., 2002):

> **S1**: AT&T: How may I help you?
> **U1**: I need to [uh] put a call on my calling card please.
> **S2**: May I have your card number please?
> **U2**: 7 6 5 4 3 2 1 0 9 8 7 6 5 4
> **S3**: What number would you like to call?
> **U3**: 8 1 4 7 7 7 6 6 6 6 (misunderstood)
> **S4**: May I have that number again?
> **U4**: 8 1 4 7 7 7 6 6 6 6
> **S5**: Thank you.

HMIHY greets users with an open-ended prompt that encourages fairly free-form spoken language input. The system determines the class of the call from a set of 14 possible classes and one additional class for tasks not covered by the system that require transfer to a human operator. The system extracts data relevant to the query either from the initial utterance or from a subdialogue. For example, given the user query *I have a query about my bill for October*, the system would classify the query as the type Ask(Bill) and extract the item Date with the value *October*. In many cases, the dialogues are short; for example, in a corpus of 4692 dialogues in several experimental trials of the system in use with real customers, 23% of the dialogues consisted of only two exchanges (Walker et al., 2002). The example shown here illustrates a more extended dialogue in which, following the classification of the call, the system enters a subdialogue to collect values for a set number of attributes relevant to this type of call. The example also illustrates how the system can recover from a misunderstood utterance (**U3–S4**).

In the next example, taken from an interaction with the MIT Mercury system that provides telephone access to an online flight database (Seneff and Polifroni, 2000), the dialogue begins with the same open-ended question and continues with questions to elicit further information from the user:

> **S1**: How may I help you?
> **U1**: I want to travel to Washington Dulles on November fourth
> **S2**: From Boston to Washington Dulles on November 4. Can you provide the approximate departure time or airline preference?

U2: I need to arrive at around nine a.m.

S3: Okay. Flights from Boston to Washington Dulles arriving at 9:00 A.M. on November 4. One moment please.

   The best matching flight is a U.S. Airways flight arriving at 8:59 A.M. I also have a United flight arriving at 8:36 A.M.

U3: What time does the United flight leave?

S4: United flight 1819 departs at 7:00 A.M. from Boston. Shall I book this flight for you?

U4: Yes please.

S5: United flight 1819 has been added to your itinerary. You depart Boston at 7:00 A.M. and arrive in Washington Dulles at 8:36 A.M. Where would you like to go next?

U5: I would like to return to Boston.

S6: What date will you be returning on?

U6: The same day.

The dialogue behavior supported by Mercury differs from that of HMIHY. Whereas in HMIHY, following the classification of the user's initial response into a call type the system takes control of the dialogue and elicits the required information from the user, in Mercury the user is also able to ask questions, as in utterance **U3**. This type of interaction is known as mixed-initiative dialogue, whereas the interaction provided by HMIHY is system-directed dialogue (see Section 2.1). The type of interaction has implications for the technologies that are used for spoken language understanding. In the HMIHY type of interaction, the first step is to identify the call type. This can be implemented using a statistical classification that determines the type of query along with named entity extraction to recognize the items in the query relevant to the class of query that has been identified. In the remainder of the dialogue, the system asks a small number of additional questions to elicit the required parameters relevant to the current call type in which the user's input is constrained to a predetermined set of response types—such as, in this example, a telephone number.

Commercial telephone-based inquiry systems are implemented using simpler technologies than those used in the Mercury system, which is a research-based application in which the aim is to explore more advanced technologies. For example, in a commercial system the dialogue is normally system-directed, where the system controls the dialogue flow, and the user responds to the system's questions. This simplifies the speech recognition process and enables the spoken language understanding module to be specified using simple grammars, while the dialogue control can consist of one or more scripts that determine the questions and the order in which they are asked. Dialogue segments that recur across different applications can also be reused. For example, there are a number of commercially available reusable dialogues for interactions such as providing an address, credit card details, dates, and so on. Different approaches to dialogue management will be discussed in more detail in Chapter 2.

1.2   BASIC ARCHITECTURE OF A SPOKEN DIALOGUE SYSTEM

The main focus of this book is on the Dialogue Manager (DM), that is, on the technologies involved in dialogue management. However, the DM is supported by a number of other components that together make up a complete dialogue system, as shown in Figure 1.1.

The flow of interaction through these components is as follows:

1. The user produces a dialogue act a, such as a query, command, or response to a system prompt, which is rendered as an acoustic signal x_u.
2. x_u is input to the Speech Recognizer component and recognized as a word string y_u with confidence score c.
3. The word string y_u (or possibly the N-best list or the word graph) is input to the SLU component and interpreted as $\tilde{a}$ with confidence score c. Note that $\tilde{a}$ is an estimate of a due to the possibility of recognition and understanding errors. It is often the case that $\tilde{a} \neq a$, that is, what the system outputs as the user's dialogue act does not correspond to what the user actually intended.
4. The system's Dialogue Context Model, which contains information about the dialogue, is updated with $(\tilde{a},c)$.
5. Given the information in the Dialogue Context Model, Dialogue Control determines the next system action, which may involve producing a system dialogue act a_s.

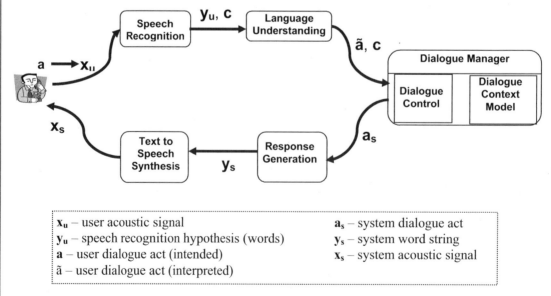

x_u – user acoustic signal
y_u – speech recognition hypothesis (words)
a – user dialogue act (intended)
$\tilde{a}$ – user dialogue act (interpreted)

a_s – system dialogue act
y_s – system word string
x_s – system acoustic signal

FIGURE 1.1: Basic spoken dialogue systems architecture.

6. The Dialogue Context Model is updated with a_s.
7. The Response Generation component converts a_s into a word string y_s.
8. y_s is rendered by the Text to Speech component as an acoustic signal x_s, which may prompt the user for further input leading to another cycle through the process.

There are many variations on how each of the components work and on the types of data that are passed between them. Many of these variations will be described in greater detail in subsequent chapters. The following sections describe the basic operations of the components in more detail.

1.2.1   Speech Understanding

The process of speech understanding typically consists of the two processes:

1. Automatic Speech Recognition (ASR)
2. Spoken Language Understanding (SLU)

ASR involves taking the acoustic signal X_u that represents what the user said and outputting a string W consisting of one or more words that represent the system's estimate of the user's utterance. ASR is a probabilistic pattern matching process and the output of the process is a set of word hypotheses, often referred to as the N-best list, or a word graph. This process can be described in terms of the following equation:

$$\hat{W} = \arg \max_{w} P\left(W \mid X\right) \qquad (1.1)$$

which states that the estimate of the best word string W involves a search over all word strings w to find the maximum value of $P(W|X)$, which is the probability of the word string W given the acoustic input X. Applying Bayes' rule, this is transformed into

$$\arg \max_{w} P\left(X \mid W\right)(W) \qquad (1.2)$$

where $P(X|W)$ is the probability of the acoustic signal X given the word string and $\hat{W}$ is computed by the *acoustic model*, which models the relationships between word strings and acoustic signals. The other component $P(W)$ is computed by the *language model*, which models the probability of sequences of words, often using n-gram language models, but in some cases using finite-state grammars. Hidden Markov models (HMMs) are typically used for acoustic modelling, whereas the language model uses either n-grams that estimate the likelihood of sequences of words or finite state grammars that model permissible word sequences. Given these two probabilities, the most likely word string W can be computed for a given acoustic signal X using an appropriate search algorithm (for a comprehensive description of speech recognition, see Jurafsky and Martin, 2008).

As noted earlier, ASR is a probabilistic process whose output may be a set of word hypotheses, often ranked in an N-best list, or a word graph. In some dialogue systems, the first-best hypothesis is chosen and passed on to SLU for further analysis. However, given that the first-best hypothesis may not be correct, there is merit in maintaining multiple recognition hypotheses so that alternatives can be considered at a later stage in the processing—for example, as a result of rescoring based on information acquired by other components of the system.

Given a string of words W from the ASR component, the SLU component analyses the string to determine its meaning (or, in many systems, the dialogue act A represented by W).

SLU is a complex process that can be carried out in a variety of ways. The traditional approach in theoretical (computational) linguistics involves two stages:

1. Syntactic analysis—to determine the constituent structure of the recognized string
2. Semantic analysis—to determine the meanings of the constituents

This approach provides a deeper level of understanding and captures fine-grained distinctions that might be missed in other approaches. In this approach, logic is often used to represent the meaning of the parsed string, with the advantage of standard mechanisms for inference, as required by the application.

However, in many spoken dialogue systems the meaning of the utterance is derived directly from the recognized string W using a *semantic grammar*. A semantic grammar uses phrase structure rules in the same way as a syntactic grammar, but the constituents in the semantic grammar are classified in terms of their function or meaning rather than in terms of syntactic categories. Generally, semantic grammars for spoken dialogue systems and other natural language understanding systems are domain-specific. So, for example, a system involving flights will have categories relevant to the flight domain, such as *airline*, *departure airport*, and *flight number*, whereas a system involving banking will have categories such as *account*, *balance*, and *transfer*. The output of the parsing of an input string using a semantic grammar is usually a set of keywords representing the main concepts being expressed in the string. A domain-specific dialogue act may also be the output of this analysis, accompanied by values extracted from the input string that fill slots in a frame. For example: the string *a flight from Belfast to Malaga* might be represented as:

Intent: Flight_reservation
DepartCity: BFS
ArrivalCity: AGP

Different methods for language understanding have been used in other types of speech-based interactive system. For example, Named Entity Extraction can be used to locate named entities within the input string where a named entity is a predefined category such as a person name, location, date, phone number, or company name that is relevant to the application. The process of named entity extraction involves associating stretches of text with the named entities. The output can be a list of named entities and their values or a dialogue act representing the user's intent along with named entities and their values. For example, the user utterance *I want credit for ten dollars* was output in the AT&T system (Gupta et al., 2006) as:

Request(Credit) monetary.amount=$10

Another approach involves the classification of utterances using a set of predefined classes. This approach has been used in call routing applications but could also be used in any application where the purpose is to determine the user's intent. The previous example illustrates this type of classification where the user's intent was identified as *Request(Credit)*. This approach is applicable where there is a relatively small and finite set of categories into which strings can be classified, and, in the case of machine learning-based approaches, where there is sufficient data to support the training of a statistical classifier. Applications such as voice search that support a large semantic space in terms of potential input are not suitable for this approach (Wang et al., 2008).

As noted earlier, the output of the SLU module may take the form of a *dialogue act*. Dialogue acts, also referred to as speech acts, conversational acts, or dialogue (or conversational) moves, represent the user's intent—for example, whether the utterance was intended as a question, command, promise, or threat. There are several classifications of dialogue acts. The Dialogue Act Markup in Several Layers (DAMSL) (Allen and Core, 1997), which has been used widely to annotate corpora of dialogues and as a basis for implementing the process of dialogue act recognition, was intended as a generic level of description in which each utterance could be tagged according to two main functions:

Forward-looking acts—for example, acts such as "statement," "action-directive," and "inforequest," which require a response

Backward-looking acts—for example, acts such as "agreement," "accept," and "acknowledge," which respond to a forward-looking act

There are also various domain-specific tagsets. For example, the project Verbmobil-1 used a set of dialogue acts that were specific to a two-party scheduling application, such as "init_date," "suggest_support_date," and "accept_date," along with a set of high-level, more general acts (Alexandersson et al., 1997).

Interpretation of dialogue acts is mainly modeled as a process of supervised classification in which classifiers are trained on a corpus of dialogues where each utterance is labeled with a dialogue act (see, e.g., Stolcke et al., 2000).

This description of the ASR and SLU components of a spoken dialogue system suggests a serial model in which the result(s) of the ASR stage are passed on to SLU for the next stage of analysis. However, there are a number of alternative approaches, one of which is to apply a stage of postprocessing of the results of the ASR stage before proceeding to SLU. Ringger and Allen (1996) use a noisy channel model of ASR errors for this task, whereas López-Cózar and Callejas (2008) use statistical models of words and contextual information to determine the corrections. It is also possible to use evidence from later stages in the interpretation process. For example, Purver et al. (2006) and Lemon and Gruenstein (2004) use combinations of features at various levels, including ASR and SLU probabilities, as well as semantic and contextual features to reorder the n-best hypotheses from the ASR stage.

1.2.2 Dialogue Manager

The DM is the central component of a spoken dialogue system, accepting interpreted input from the ASR and SLU components, interacting with external knowledge sources, producing messages to be output to the user, and generally controlling the dialogue flow. DM can be seen as consisting of two components:

> *Dialogue Context Model*—Keeping track of information relevant to the dialogue in order to support the process of dialogue management. This may include information about what has been said so far in the dialogue and the extent to which this information is grounded, that is, shared between the system and the user.
> *Dialogue Control*—Deciding what to do next in the context of the current dialogue context. Decisions may include prompting the user for more input, clarifying or grounding the user's previous input, or outputting some information to the user.

Dialogue Management will be described in greater detail in Chapter 2 and illustrated with examples throughout the book.

1.2.3 System Output

Generally, the generation of the system's output has received less attention in the research literature in comparison with the effort devoted to the interpretation of the user's input. As shown in Figure 1.1, output generation consists of Response Generation, in which the message a_s to be spoken to the user is constructed as a string of words y_s, and Text-to-Speech Synthesis (TTS), in which y_s is synthesized as an acoustic signal x_s and output as speech.

In most commercial systems, response generation is a fairly trivial task involving inserting items retrieved from the database into a predefined response template. Nevertheless, considerable effort is devoted to issues such as prompt design, since the quality of the system's output can have a major impact on the user's acceptance of the system, whereas carefully designed prompts also play an important role in constraining the user's response and thus supporting the ASR and SLU processes (Cohen et al., 2004).

Response generation can be viewed as two tasks: content planning and content realization. Content planning involves issues such as (1) how to determine what to say by selecting and ranking options from the content to be expressed; (2) planning the use of discourse relations such as comparison and contrast, in order to present the information in a meaningful manner; and (3) adapting the information to the user's perceived needs and preferences. Content realization is concerned with how to express the content in terms of grouping different propositions into clauses and sentences, generating appropriate referring expressions, and using appropriate discourse cues. For an overview of recent approaches to response generation for spoken dialogue systems, see Jokinen and Wilcock (2001) and Demberg and Moore (2006).

Outputting the system's messages y_s as spoken utterances x_s can involve either TTS or the use of prerecorded prompts. TTS is applicable for messages that are dynamically constructed and that cannot be predicted in advance. In general, the quality of TTS engines has improved considerably over the past decade so that output using TTS is not only easy to comprehend, but also satisfying for the user. Commercial systems use prerecorded prompts where possible, as these are more realistic and humanlike. It is also possible to concatenate short items of prerecorded text into longer messages, although this requires careful consideration of issues such as intonation and timing, in order not to sound jerky and unnatural.

1.3 APPLICATION DOMAINS FOR SPOKEN DIALOGUE SYSTEMS

Since the early 1990s, a large number of spoken dialogue systems have been developed in the commercial domain to support telephone-based services and transactions. The main motivation behind these applications is that they provide access to electronic databases so that the user can search for information using natural language expressions and clarification dialogues. Often, the information is Web-based and the service requires that the user dials a telephone number to interact with an application. Spoken dialogue systems are also being used in other environments, such as in-car entertainment and navigation systems, or smart home applications. Some typical application domains are shown in Table 1.1.

Call routing was illustrated earlier with an example from the HMIHY system. Troubleshooting is similar to call routing in that the first step is to classify the reason for the call from the set of possible cases that the system can handle. However, troubleshooting is typically more complex than call routing as callers are often unable to provide a precise description of the fault and it may also be

TABLE 1.1: Application domains for goal-oriented spoken dialogue systems.

Call routing
Troubleshooting
Directory assistance
Telephone-based enquiries, e.g., travel/hotel/car rental enquiries, bank balance

Desktop information assistance
Training applications
Educational and tutoring applications
Robot control
Planning assistance
Information acquisition
Healthcare systems, e.g., patient monitoring
Car systems
Smart home applications
Ubiquitous applications

difficult for the system to instruct nontechnical callers in how to perform a troubleshooting action (Acomb et al., 2007). Moreover, in a troubleshooting application callers do not typically describe the actual problem (e.g., "The modem is wrongly configured"), but instead describe the symptoms of the problem (e.g., "I can't connect to the Internet"). For this reason, rather than mapping from a small set of expressions to a predetermined set of categories, as in call routing, in troubleshooting a more extensive natural language processing solution is required that can relate descriptions of problems and symptoms at various degrees of specificity to categories that are relevant to troubleshooting within the particular application.

Many of the other types of systems listed in Table 1.1 involve retrieving information from a database using a spoken dialogue. The interaction is similar to form-filling in which the system elicits values for all the required attributes from the user, looks up the database to retrieve relevant records, and then speaks these records out to the user. These types of system have been used widely in industrial applications since the interaction can be modeled using constrained questions and grammars, which leads to higher recognition accuracy and consequently higher task completion rates. Indeed, accuracy has often been found to be the most important correlate of user satisfaction (see Section 1.5).

In addition to retrieving information, dialogue systems may also perform a transaction, for example, making a booking using a credit card, or transferring money between bank accounts. The same technologies are involved (such as extracting values for source and destination accounts), but in this case the transaction results in changes to the application database.

Healthcare is an important new domain for spoken dialogue applications. In some cases, applications may provide basic information to patients, for example, about their insurance entitlement or their upcoming appointments. Other applications support self-monitoring, where patients can input relevant data and obtain feedback on their condition. One example of such a system is DI@L-log, a system for home monitoring of patients with type 2 diabetes (Black et al., 2005). DI@L-log enables patients to speak their vital signs health data (weight, blood sugar, and blood pressure) using speech or DTMF (telephone keypad). Data are retrieved from the back-end system during a call and at the end of the call the database is updated with the newly elicited readings. The system provides feedback by comparing the new data with readings from previous calls as well as target readings determined by the clinician. A rule-based decision support component modeled on medical protocols gives feedback to the patients and, in the case of problem situations, sends an alert to the clinician. Levin and Levin (2006) describe a similar system for the assessment and monitoring of chronic pain, whereas in the European Union (EU)-funded HOMEY project a more extended dialogue between the system and a patient supports the management of conditions such as hypertension and breast cancer (Giorgino et al., 2005).

Spoken dialogue technology is being increasingly applied in other types of applications and environments that go beyond telephone-based interactions. There are a number of systems currently under development for use in vehicles in hands busy/eyes busy situations—for example, to support navigation, provide relevant information as in telephone-based systems, and control in-car systems for entertainment. These systems tend to be user-driven in that they provide responses to user queries and commands, but can involve fairly complex spoken language understanding given that the user input is not constrained by a system question. The following example is taken from the Conversational Helper for Automotive Tasks (CHAT) system, which provides a spoken dialogue interface to three different applications: MP3 player, restaurant finder, and navigation (Weng et al., 2007b):

U: Switch to restaurant.
S: OK, switched to the restaurant finder.
U: Can you find me a Chinese restaurant in Palo Alto with good service?
S: There are 11 Chinese restaurants in Palo Alto with good service.

. . .

U: Switch to navigation.

S: OK, switched to navigation.

U: Take me to Little Garden Restaurant, but stop by Bosch Page Mill Office.

. . .

U: Switch to music player.

S: OK, switched to MP3 music player.

U: What songs do you have by Alicia Keys?

One of the problems faced by systems such as CHAT is that, in addition to speech recognition errors that occur in noisy environments such as the car, users have to interact with the system while they are engaged in the primary task of driving. Moreover, users typically do not provide precise and complete names for locations, restaurants, and items of entertainment, so the language understanding system has to be able to handle imperfect input and map it on to items in the relevant domains.

Applications are also being developed that support independent living by providing information and services in smart homes, often for users with disabilities. Thus, the dialogue system might help users control their environment, switching on lights and operating household equipment using spoken language commands, and engaging in dialogue to resolve ambiguities or discuss problems (Montoro et al., 2004; Pérez et al., 2006).

Ubiquitous applications, in which people "on the move" engage with spoken dialogue applications, provide a particular challenge as they require different interaction paradigms compared with traditional systems (Weiser, 1991). For example, although traditional applications involve a single user in turn-based communication with the system on the computer or on the telephone, ubiquitous applications may involve several users and devices engaged in open-ended and dynamically constructed concurrent dialogues. Thus, dialogues in ubiquitous (also called pervasive) applications will tend to be distributed across different physical locations as the user moves from one place to another, and they will also involve different devices that are available in different locations. For example, when a user interacts with the system in his office and then goes to a meeting room and continues the interaction there, the dialogue may be managed by different dialogue components due to the change in setting and possibly also changes in the device used to conduct the dialogue and display system output (Turunen et al., 2006). Similarly, if the user goes outside or drives the car, different devices and different DMs will be involved. A challenge for dialogue management in ubiquitous spoken language applications is to present a consistent and unified dialogue to the user. Some of these issues have been explored in recent research projects such as SmartKom (Wahlster 2006) and TALK (http://www.talk-project.org/).

Spoken dialogue systems are also being developed for educational purposes. For example, there are systems under development that act as interfaces for intelligent tutoring systems enabling them to provide individualized instruction using a more natural interface than keyboard input (see, e.g., Litman and Forbes-Riley, 2005).

A particularly challenging area is spoken dialogue interaction with physically embodied agents, such as robots, since in this case the interaction focuses on a physical environment in which the robot moves and manipulates objects. Additional components are required to represent and reason about the physical environment. For example, the robot Godot, developed at the University of Edinburgh, moves around the basement of the department using an internal map for navigation (Bos et al., 2003). The robot engages in dialogue with users about its position and current environment. Another example is the robot Fritz (Bennewitz et al., 2007), which engages humans in multimodal dialogues, that is, besides speech gestures can also be used.

Finally, an emerging application area is the use of spoken dialogue technology in computer games. Most prominent games consoles offer games with speech input and output, mainly to support action commands. Some recent research has been investigating the use of spoken dialogue systems to help children interact with animated characters in a fairy tale-based video game (Gustafson et al., 2005; Mehta and Corradini, 2006). The robust understanding of children's speech is a major challenge for these systems. Additional challenges include how to specify virtual worlds and embodied characters, and the nature of dialogue management for complex, multimodal edutainment applications.

1.4   DATA COLLECTION AND DIALOGUE CORPORA

A corpus is a machine-readable collection of speech or text that can be used to count the frequencies, types, and contexts of occurrences of particular phenomena of interest for the purposes of analysis, as a basis for the design of a new application, as a resource for data-driven approaches based on machine learning, and as a tool for evaluation. One of the first corpora of spoken dialogues is the Switchboard corpus, which consists of telephone conversations between strangers collected in the early 1990s, containing 2430 conversations, and totaling 240 hours of speech (Godfrey et al., 1992). Corpora have been collected within numerous research projects on spoken dialogue, such as the DARPA Communicator project (Walker et al., 2001). Companies deploying spoken dialogue applications also collect recordings of interactions for the purposes of monitoring the performance of the system and determining future improvements.

Creating a corpus of dialogues involves recording the dialogues and then transcribing and annotating them. Transcriptions may be orthographic or some phonetic notation may be used to represent pronunciation and possibly also prosodic information. Much effort has thus been put into standardizing representations and data formats. Extensible Markup Language (XML) and its extension to multimodal coding, Extensible MultiModal Annotation markup language (EMMA) are widely used as formats for data representation, although they do not specify how the transcription should be done. For annotation, a markup language may be used. For example, the Text Encoding Initiative produced a markup format for transcribed speech (Johansson, 1995), whereas annotation tools have been developed such as Dialogue Annotation Tool (Allen and Core, 1997). Usually, practical systems use their own classifications for discourse information but standardized coding schemes, especially for dialogue acts, have also been studied. For instance, the Maptask coding scheme (Carletta et al., 1996) used dialogue moves and games as the general basis for dialogue coding, whereas the DAMSL dialogue act classification (Allen and Core, 1997) is used in Switchboard (Jurafsky et al., 1997). An example of an annotation that pays special attention to dialogue strategy optimization and user simulations is presented by Georgila et al. (2005). This is an automatic annotation system for the COMMUNICATOR human–machine dialogue data, and it produces annotations that build up Information State Update style representations (see Chapter 4) of the current dialogue context after every user or system utterance. The types of context information are divided into five levels: dialogue level, task level, low level, history level, and reward level, the latter being especially coded for reinforcement learning experiments (see Chapter 2).

Data collection involves deciding what to collect and how to collect it. It is important to collect samples of dialogue that are representative of the application to be developed — for example, a spoken dialogue system for making flight reservations may share some aspects of a system for hotel reservations or one for theater bookings, but there will also be differences in terms of vocabulary, data types, and dialogue flow. Recordings of human–human conversations, such as recordings made by call centers, could be used to inform the design of applications to be used in the automation of some call center interactions. However, since human–human and human–computer interactions are dissimilar, for example, interactions with a computer are typically more constrained, particularly because of the potentially high error rates of the ASR module, human–human interactions cannot as such be modeled in spoken dialogue systems. There is also some evidence that humans behave differently when they are aware that they are interacting with machines rather than other humans (Doran et al., 2001).

One way to address this issue is to collect simulated human–computer dialogues using the Wizard of Oz (WOZ) method (Fraser and Gilbert 1991). In a typical WOZ setup, the human user believes that they are interacting with a machine but in fact the machine's operations are simulated in whole or in part by a human operator (or wizard). The output of the wizard can be made to appear more machinelike by using TTS. It is more difficult, however, to simulate the performance of the ASR module, as the types of errors made by ASR are not necessarily similar to those made by humans. Recently, this has been addressed by introducing artificial noise into the interaction in order to simulate the noise produced by the ASR and SLU components (Rieser et al., 2005).

Data collection using WOZ and similar methods is expensive in terms of the time and effort required by the humans who take part in the interactions. For this reason, user simulators are being increasingly used to take the place of real users and to engage in interactions with a dialogue system by generating responses to the system's prompts. In this way, large corpora of dialogues can be collected without the involvement of human users in the process. Simulated data can be used to evaluate different aspects of a dialogue system, particularly at the earlier stages of development, or to determine the effects of changes to the system's functionalities. For example, in order to evaluate the consequences of the choice of a particular confirmation strategy on transaction duration or user satisfaction, simulations can be done using different strategies and the resulting data can be analyzed and comparisons made between the strategies used. Another example would be the introduction of errors or unpredicted answers in order to evaluate the capacity of the DM to react to unexpected situations.

Early user simulators were rule-based, in that the actions of the simulated user are specified by rules that determine the user's actions across a range of scenarios (López-Cózar et al., 2003). The advantage of this method is that the investigator has complete control over the design of the evaluation study, whereas the downside is that the user actions prescribed by the rules may not be representative of the complete range of actions to be found in data collected from interactions with real users. An alternative method is to develop statistical models of the user in which user action probabilities are learned from dialogue corpora following which the model is used to simulate dialogues with the dialogue system. For a recent overview of user simulation methods, see Shatzmann et al. (2006).

1.5   EVALUATING SPOKEN DIALOGUE SYSTEMS

Evaluation is an essential part of a dialogue system's design and development process, especially when the technology is deployed to build practical applications. For systems that will be used with real users in real situations, usefulness and usability are pertinent issues. However, although evaluation has always been important in system development, there are no generally applicable metrics or methodologies that could be used across tasks and systems. Moreover, evaluation can be done for several purposes and by different interest groups, so the goals and starting points can differ considerably. System developers and researchers mainly engage themselves in system performance, whereas interface designers are usually interested in user evaluations. Both types of evaluation are an important means to assess the dialogue system's usefulness and usability. Evaluation can also be organized to assess the current state of technology in the form of surveys and roadmaps to guide further development, whereas companies and service providers regularly perform evaluation in the form of market surveys and ordinary users evaluate systems for their own interests. Nowadays, various evaluation challenges have also become common, starting from the written language understanding systems (MUC, TREC), to recent generation component challenges (GIVE).

Intuitively, a dialogue system should be preferred to another one if it enables interactions with the user in a natural and efficient manner. For instance, comparing the two dialogues in Figures 1.2

S: Good day. Welcome to the train timetable service. Where would you like to start your train journey from?
U: Helsinki.
S: From Helsinki. Where would you like to go to from Helsinki?
U: Tampere.
S: Tampere. And when would you like to go from Helsinki to Tampere?
U: Today after 11 pm.
S: Today after 11 pm. There are no trains from Helsinki to Tampere after 11pm.

FIGURE 1.2: Dialogue 1.

and 1.3, we can summarize some of the main differences between the sample dialogues in Table 1.2. Some of the features are considered characteristic of "good" and "bad" dialogues, and consequently of "good" and "bad" dialogue systems.

However, instead of just providing descriptive, and in many cases subjective, accounts of the differences between the dialogue features (style, efficiency, helpfulness), dialogue strategies (initiative, confirmation, feedback), or observable dialogue properties (length, word error rate, task completion rate), we would also want to have quantitative measures of the dialogues and dialogue systems so as to support our judgments with more objective comparison results. We would like to have objective answers to such questions as how to measure task complexity and dialogue success, how does the number of errors and misunderstandings affect the user's satisfaction, what is the impact of changes in the components on system performance as a whole, etc. The decision method should be reliable and robust in predicting task completion and user satisfaction with respect to the chosen evaluation metrics, and the parameters should be able to pin down the features that distinguish good system performance. It would be good if the parameters would also be able to predict similar satisfaction rates with respect to future systems, given that the systems show similar characteristics. It may not always be possible to test user satisfaction and task completion (e.g., the setup is too expensive or impractical at a given situation), and so it would be useful to try to predict these

S: Good day. Welcome to the train timetable service. How may I help you?
U: I would like to go to Tampere today after 11pm.
S: Ok. Where would you depart from?
U: Helsinki.
S: Sorry. There are no trains from Helsinki to Tampere today after 11pm. The last train departs at 10.10 pm. The first train departs at 6.30am.

FIGURE 1.3: Dialogue 2.

TABLE 1.2: Some differences between the dialogues.

ASPECT	DIALOGUE 2.1	DIALOGUE 2.2
Style	Mechanical	Natural
Efficiency	Less	More
Helpfulness	No	Yes
Initiative	System	Mixed
Confirmation	Explicit	Implicit
Feedback	No	Yes
Dialogue length	Longer	Shorter
Word Error Rate	Lower	Higher
Task completion rate	Better	Lower
Natualness	Lower	Higher

quantities from the other observable quantities that are easier (and cheaper) to measure. We would thus ideally like to have a principled way to decide, on the basis of the measurements, which of the systems would give higher user satisfaction, and which could thus be favored over the other.

Moreover, the evaluation method should also be applicable to various tasks and applications so as to allow comparisons among different types of dialogue systems. These requirements, however, presuppose task analysis and understanding of how the different system components contribute to task completion. A standardized task representation (e.g., an attribute–value matrix) can provide a means to normalize over task complexity, and standardized system architectures can be used to capture variability in applications. However, open or unspecified tasks do not lend themselves to representations that presuppose precise task definitions. Evaluation of conversational and/or multimodal dialogue systems that support this type of advanced versatile task management would thus require a task taxonomy that would allow presentation of task complexity and comparison of tasks along measurable uniform task parameters. This type of task taxonomy seems very difficult to produce, especially when considering complex tasks in rich communicative environments.

In practice, setting up a full-scale system evaluation requires careful planning and preparation. Besides the necessary logistics, practical arrangements, and recruitment of test users, it is important to consider the overall purpose of the enterprise. Three issues need to be considered in order to structure the evaluation task appropriately: the goals, the metrics, and the methods. The evaluation criteria specify which particular properties of system performance can be identified with the goals, and to decide whether the goals have been achieved. Appropriate metrics to measure these properties need to be determined, as well as methods of how the values for these metrics are assigned. In the evaluation frameworks, the metrics are related to task completion, dialogue success, and user satisfaction. Evaluation will be discussed in more detail in Chapter 6.

1.6 SOFTWARE AND TOOLKITS FOR SPOKEN DIALOGUE SYSTEMS DEVELOPMENT

Developing a spoken dialogue system requires the integration of the various components shown in Figure 1.1. Fortunately, a number of toolkits have been produced that help to reduce this effort by providing off-the-shelf or easily adapted component technologies. Some toolkits and platforms are available free of charge, usually under a special license agreement for academic and educational usage, whereas others are commercial products developed within particular companies working in the area of deployed speech systems.

1.6.1 Academic Systems

One of the first toolkits to become freely available was the CSLU toolkit, which was developed at the Center for Spoken Language Understanding (CSLU) at the Oregon Graduate Institute of Science and Technology with the aim of supporting learning and research in speech and language (Cole, 1999; http://cslu.cse.ogi.edu/). The toolkit includes core technologies for speech recognition and TTS along with a graphical authoring tool, Rapid Application Developer (RAD), to support the design and implementation of spoken dialogue systems. Building a dialogue system with RAD involves selecting and linking graphical dialogue objects into a graph-based dialogue system (see Chapter 2). RAD is a relatively simple tool to use and is thus useful for introducing dialogue system concepts. More complex applications can be built by linking RAD with a database or with information on the World Wide Web (see McTear, 2004, for a tutorial on the use of RAD for such applications). The use of a graphical tool to specify the call flow of spoken dialogue systems has now been extended to a number of commercially available dialogue systems development platforms. Although RAD remains an interesting tool to use for educational purposes, it has been largely superseded by platforms that have been designed specifically for Web-based applications, such as those supporting VoiceXML (see Chapter 2).

A wide range of toolkits have been developed within academic research centers, often with the purpose of supporting the implementation of particular theories of dialogue. Only a few of these toolkits can be mentioned here. References to a wide range of toolkits can be found at various websites such as the Wikipedia article on spoken dialogue systems (http://en.wikipedia.org/wiki/

Dialog_system) and the web pages associated with the textbook (McTear, 2004); see http://www.infj.ulst.ac.uk/sdt/.

The Olympus architecture was developed at Carnegie Mellon University to support researchers in spoken dialogue systems (Bohus et al., 2007). Like the CSLU toolkit, Olympus incorporates modules required for spoken dialogue systems. Dialogue management is handled by Ravenclaw (Bohus and Rudnicky, 2003), whereas for ASR various speech recognition engines from the Sphinx series are supported (http://cmusphinx.sourceforge.net/html/cmusphinx.php). Natural language understanding is handled by the Phoenix parser (Ward and Issar, 1994), natural language generation uses Rosetta, which is a template-based system (Oh and Rudnicky, 2000), and the TTS interface supports the use of various TTS engines such as Festival (http://www.cstr.ed.ac.uk/projects/festival/) and Cepstral Swift (http://cepstral.com/). For further details, see http://www.ravenclaw-olympus.org/.

Web-Accessible Multimodal Interfaces (WAMI), a toolkit that has recently become available, makes use of web programming techniques for the development of spoken and multimodal dialogue systems requiring modules for ASR, TTS, and SLU (Gruenstein et al., 2008; http://wami.csail.mit.edu/). The WAMI portal also provides access to MIT's speech recognition engine as a web service. An iPhone WAMI Browser, which allows iPhone users interact with any WAMI-enabled website, is currently being tested. The WAMI web page provides videos as well as links to applications, including a Google Maps system.

Finally, within academic systems a new set of tools is being developed within the EU-funded project CLASSIC (http://www.classic-project.org/) that will provide an architecture for a unified end-to-end statistical model of uncertainty in spoken dialogue systems.

1.6.2   VoiceXML Platforms

VoiceXML is a markup language based on XML for creating spoken dialog systems using standard web programming techniques and languages (see Chapter 2). A range of platforms have been made available for developers. There are two main options:

1.   Standalone systems that run on PCs and servers, for example:
   • IBM WebSphere Voice Toolkit (http://www-01.ibm.com/software/pervasive/voice_toolkit/)
   • Voxeo Prophecy (http://www.voxeo.com/prophecy/)
   • Nuance Voice Platform (http://www.nuance.com/voiceplatform/)
   • Voxpilot Open Media Platform (http://www.voxpilot.com/)

- Loquendo VoxNauta (http://www.loquendo.com)
- Avaya Dialog Designer (http://www.avaya.com/gcm/master-usa/en-us/products/ offers/dialog_designer.htm)

2. Web-based environments, for example:
- Nuance Cafe (previously BeVocal Cafe) (http://www.nuance.com/care/solutions/ ondemand/cafe/)
- Voxeo Evolution (http://evolution.voxeo.com/)
- Tellme (http://www.tellme.com/)
- Loquendo Cafe (http://www.loquendocafe.com/index.asp)
- Voice Genie (http://www.genesyslab.com/voicegenie/)

Further information about VoiceXML products can be found at http://www.w3.org/Voice/ #implementations and http://www.vxmldirectory.com/index.php?title=VoiceXML_Platforms.

1.6.3   Voice Systems on Mobile Devices
A recent trend is for voice interfaces to be available on mobile devices that provide voice search and various other information services such as weather, traffic, and movies. These include:

- Microsoft Live Search (http://www.loco4local.com/)
- Nuance Mobile Search (http://www.nuance.com/mobilesearch)
- V-Lingo Mobile (http://www.vlingomobile.com/)
- Google 411 (http://www.google.com/goog411/)
- Tellme (http://www.tellme.com/you)

1.6.4   Individual Components
Individual components for speech-based applications are often used for development and integration into spoken dialogue systems. In addition to the various components mentioned earlier that have been incorporated into the Olympus system, the following are widely used resources:

- HTK—the HMM toolkit, which is used at many sites worldwide, mainly for speech recognition research but also for research into speech synthesis, character recognition, and DNA sequencing (http://htk.eng.cam.ac.uk/)
- Stanford Natural Language Processing Group has developed tools such as a probabilistic parser (Stanford Parser), part-of-speech tagger (Stanford POS Tagger), Stanford Named Entity Recognizer, and the Stanford Classifier (http://www-nlp.stanford.edu/software/ index.shtml)
- Microsoft Speech tools (http://www.microsoft.com/speech/speech2007/default.mspx)

1.7   SUMMARY

This chapter has provided an introduction to spoken dialogue systems and illustrated, with some examples, a generic architecture with the different components of a spoken dialogue application as well as the processes involved in a dialogue cycle through the system components. Different types of spoken dialogue system were discussed, including task-based systems for call routing, information retrieval, and various types of transactions, such as travel and hotel reservations. Methods for collecting dialogue data as well as constructing and using dialogue corpora were discussed, and the issues concerning dialogue systems evaluation were presented. The chapter concludes with an overview of some toolkits and software products.

The next chapter will take a more detailed look at dialogue management, examining the issues involved in dialogue control and dialogue modeling, and reviewing a number of approaches that have been taken to design and handcraft the dialogue management component. Moreover, recent approaches involving machine learning from data will be reviewed. VoiceXML, a Web-based standard for spoken dialogue systems development, will also be introduced.

·   ·   ·   ·   ·

CHAPTER 2

Dialogue Management

The Dialogue Manager (DM) is the central component of a spoken dialogue system, controlling the interaction with the user and communicating with external knowledge sources. Dialogue management is often viewed in terms of two subcomponents: dialogue control, which deals with the flow of control in the dialogue, and dialogue context modeling, which is concerned with contextual information used by the DM to interpret the user's input and inform the decisions of the dialogue control component. A number of methods for implementing dialogue control are discussed, in particular graph-based and frame-based methods, followed by an overview of VoiceXML, which supports these types of dialogue control, will be presented. The second part of the chapter addresses the issue of dialogue modeling, which involves keeping track of the state of the dialogue, and more generally, maintaining a representation of those aspects of the context that are relevant to dialogue management. The chapter concludes with an overview of an alternative approach to dialogue management involving statistical and machine learning methods that is becoming increasingly popular in current dialogue research.

2.1   DIALOGUE CONTROL

Dialogue control involves deciding what to do next once the user's input has been received and interpreted. Examples of decisions include:

- Prompting the user for more input
- Clarifying or grounding the user's previous input
- Outputting some information to the user

These decisions are often prescribed, with choices based on factors such as the confidence levels associated with the user's input. For example, if the confidence levels are above a certain threshold, the system can assume that it has correctly interpreted the input and can proceed to its next action, whereas if the levels are low it may first try to verify that it has interpreted the input correctly or even ask the user to repeat their utterance. Decisions such as these can be anticipated at design time and hard-coded into the dialogue control. However, other methods of dialogue control may require decisions that are taken dynamically, based, for example, on reasoning about the current dialogue state and using evidence from a combination of different domain and dialogue knowledge sources. Thus, in addition to confidence scores from the Automatic Speech Recognition (ASR) and Spoken Language Understanding (SLU) components, the DM may also take other factors into account such as the relative importance of the information that has been elicited, what needs to be achieved in the task at hand, the user's needs and preferences, and the history of the dialogue so far. There may also be mechanisms to enable the system to adapt its output and style of interaction to different users, as well as sophisticated ways of detecting and handling errors.

Most commercial systems use simple dialogue modeling and dialogue control techniques, which are generally appropriate for the types of application being deployed. Here, the essential requirement is to be able to complete a transaction successfully and efficiently. Chapter 4 will present examples of several systems that aim to provide a more natural "conversational" style of interaction and also to engage in more complex tasks than are currently addressed in deployed applications.

There are various methods for implementing dialogue control:

1. Use of graphs
2. Use of frames
3. Use of plan-based and other approaches based mainly on methods derived from Artificial Intelligence (AI)
4. Use of statistical models

Dialogue control using graphs, frames, and statistical models will be illustrated in the next sections, whereas plan-based and other AI-based approaches will be discussed in Chapter 4.

2.1.1 Graphs

In dialogue control based on graphs, the actions that can be taken at each point (or state) of the dialogue are depicted in a graph (or call flow diagram). This method is also known as "finite-state based" dialogue control since the states of the dialogue graph can be traversed using a finite state automaton. Figure 2.1 presents a portion of a dialogue graph that elicits a destination and a day, and also confirms the values elicited.

The nodes of the graph represent the system's questions, the transitions between the nodes represent answers to the questions, and the graph specifies all legal dialogues. Alternatively, each stage in the dialogue can be viewed as a state in which some dialogue action is performed—for example, information is elicited from or confirmed with the user, or some action is performed by

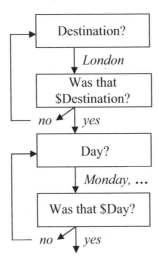

FIGURE 2.1: A dialogue graph.

the system. Graphs have widely been used to design dialogue systems and there are several toolkits, such as the Center for Spoken Language Understanding (CSLU) toolkit (Cole, 1999), and various commercial toolkits that allow designers to construct a dialogue by dragging, dropping, and connecting icons representing dialogue objects on the screen. The toolkit then compiles the graph into a language such as VoiceXML, which can be interpreted and run as a dialogue application (see Section 2.3 on dialogue control and dialogue modeling using VoiceXML).

The management of dialogue control is fairly simple in graph-based systems since transitions to a next node are predetermined and based on a small set of conditions, such as whether the user's utterance was understood with a sufficient degree of confidence. Use of graphs is suitable for fairly simple interactions where the dialogue flow can be predetermined. Once the dialogue becomes more complex, the number of nodes and transitions increases rapidly and it is no longer possible to build the graph manually. For example, given five items of information to be elicited, each with three possible values (unknown, known, verified), 3^5 nodes would be required, giving rise to an even larger number of transitions.

Thus, graph-based dialogue design is appropriate for well-structured tasks in which there is a predetermined set of questions to be asked, as in questionnaires and form-filling. Moreover, since the space of user responses to each prompt can be predicted, the speech recognition and language understanding grammars can be restricted to what the user is expected to say following each prompt, thus enhancing the performance of the ASR and SLU components. Response generation is also simpler since in confirmations the system can reflect back the information provided by the user in the previous utterance and gather together the information retrieved from the database into a predefined template.

Dialogues developed using the graph-based method support a style of interaction known as system-directed (or system initiative) dialogue. In this type of interaction, the system prompts the user for one or more items of information. The system might confirm that it has correctly understood each item as it is elicited, or may leave confirmation until some or all of the items have been collected. Once all the information has been gathered, the system performs some task, such as retrieving the required data, and then outputs this information to the user. The user has little or no control over the dialogue flow and is mainly restricted to responding to the system's prompts, although there are often options for "go back" or "start over" that allow the user to take some degree of control over the interaction. Generally, however, system-directed dialogues are relatively rigid and inflexible. They follow a predetermined path and the user cannot take the initiative to correct items that the system has misrecognized, or introduce new information or topics that have not been predicted at design time. Thus, system-directed dialogues would not be suitable for more complex tasks such as planning a holiday that involve negotiation of constraints that had not been predicted in advance by the system designer and included in the dialogue graph.

2.1.2 Frames

Frames offer a way of providing more flexibility to dialogue control. A frame represents the information that the system has to elicit in the course of the dialogue. Frames consist of slots that are filled with the values elicited from the user. The first example below is of a frame at the beginning of an interaction, whereas the second example shows the state of the system part way through the interaction:

(1)
destination: unknown
date: unknown
time of departure: unknown
(2)
destination: London
date: unknown
time of departure: 9

Frames such as these can be used to direct the dialogue flow. At the beginning of the dialogue, represented by frame (1), the system can ask for any of the items that have the value "unknown." Depending on how the dialogue control is implemented, the system might ask for each item separately and in the order listed in the frame. At the point in the dialogue represented by frame (2), the system should only ask for any items that are unknown, in this case, the date.

Frames are used to support more flexible dialogues by allowing the user to fill in the slots in different orders and different combinations. For example, if the user responds to the system's initial prompt with a destination and a time of departure, these slots are then filled, as in frame (2), and the system can ask for any further items that are still unknown. This style of input is referred to as "over-answering," where the user provides more information than is requested in the system prompt, as in:

S1: Where are you flying to?
U1: London, departing at 9.

Over-answering is not possible in a graph-based dialogue because each system prompt is explicitly linked to a range of responses that in turn lead to the next system prompt. Thus, in a graph-based system, a response such as **S1** would expect a word or phrase stating a destination as a response. If the user produced an utterance such as **U1**, this additional information would either be ignored or misrecognized. Indeed, the consequences could be even worse, as the system would subsequently ask the next question in the graph—that is, "What time do you wish to depart?"—which would be inappropriate given that the user had already provided this information.

Interpretation of the user's input in frame-based systems is more complex compared with graph-based systems as the user's utterance can include various permutations of the required information. For example, in response to the question "Where are you flying to?," the user may respond with an utterance containing items such as:

Destination
Destination + Date
Destination + Time
Destination + Date + Time
etc.

More complex grammars would be required in which all of the items relevant to the dialogue can be extracted from the user's utterance to fill slots in a frame. Semantic grammars are often used for this purpose because they focus on the semantic content of the input rather than its syntactic structure. They are also more robust to the types of ungrammatical input and recognition errors that occur in spontaneous speech. See, for example, the Phoenix parser (Ward and Issar, 1994), which is designed to enable robust parsing of such input and has been used in a number of spoken dialogue systems. Similar methods have been used in a wide range of semantics-based parsers for spoken dialogue systems (e.g., Seneff, 1992; Torres et al., 2005).

In addition to permitting a wider range of user input, the use of frames provides for a more flexible dialogue flow since the dialogue can be driven by the information needed at a given state in the dialogue and actions to fill slots can be executed in various sequences. This flexibility is desirable for applications that permit more flexible slot-filling and in which it is desirable to allow the users more freedom in how they input information to the system.

However, frame-based systems require a more elaborate dialogue control algorithm to determine what the system's next question should be based on the information in the current frame. In VoiceXML, this is managed by the Form Interpretation Algorithm (FIA) (see next section). Other systems have used various rule-based methods to determine dialogue control. For example, in the Philips SpeechMania dialogue architecture, which was used in the Philips Train Timetable Information System (Aust el al., 1995), a declarative approach was adopted in which each question was listed along with its preconditions (what have to be true for the question to be asked), as in:

condition: unknown(origin) & unknown(destination)
question: "Which route do you want to travel?"

condition: unknown(origin)
question: "Where do you want to travel from?"

condition: unknown(destination)
question: "Where do you want to travel to?"

The dialogue control algorithm functioned as a production system that looped through all the questions and selected the first question for which the conditions were true. In this manner, the dialogue developed dynamically based on the current state of the system, resulting in a more natural and more flexible interaction.

Similar frame-based methods have been used widely, for example, in the CU Communicator (Pellom et al., 2001) and the Queen's Communicator (Hanna et al., 2007). A more complex type of data structure, the E-form (electronic form) was used in the MIT spoken dialogue systems (Goddeau et al., 1996). In E-forms, slots can have different priorities to reflect different user preferences and relations between slot items. In the CMU Communicator, a hierarchical data structure, known as a product tree, was used to represent an itinerary (Rudnicky et al., 1999). The product tree is constructed dynamically over the course of an interaction, giving flexibility to the dialogue, for example, allowing additional legs to be added to the itinerary and also enabling the focus of the dialogue to be easily shifted.

2.2 DIALOGUE MODELING

The term "dialogue modeling" is used in two different ways in the literature. On one hand, it is used to refer to the modeling of the whole process of dialogic interaction, involving phenomena such as turn-taking, cooperation and communicative competence, dialogue coherence—indeed, all of those phenomena that contribute to participation in dialogue. Dialogue modeling in this sense provides a gold standard for researchers interested in simulating human dialogue processes, whether in the interests of AI research in general or as a basis for the development of more humanlike spoken dialogue interfaces.

The second use of the term specifically refers to information about the dialogue that is modeled to support the processes of interpretation and dialogue control. Various terms have been used to describe this information, such as the "dialogue model," "system state," "dialogue context," or "information state." Here, the term "dialogue context model" will be used.

In the next subsection, the types of information represented in the dialogue context model will be discussed. A more advanced representation, known as Information State Theory, will be introduced in Chapter 4, while the modeling of dialogue phenomena will be discussed in Chapter 5.

2.2.1   Dialogue Context Model

Modeling the ongoing dialogue involves keeping track of what has been said so far in the dialogue and interpreting the user's input in the light of this information. As described in Chapter 1, interpretation of the user's input involves taking the outputs from the ASR and SLU components and processing them to determine the user's meaning and intentions. In many systems, interpretation is a simple process of extracting items from the ASR and SLU outputs to create a database query. In these systems, data are passed in a pipeline fashion, beginning with the output of the ASR, often in the form of a string of words representing the recognizer's best hypothesis. This is then processed by the SLU and the resulting semantic interpretation is passed to the DM. However, interpretation may also involve a more complex process requiring resolution of ellipsis and anaphoric reference, and taking into account information from the overall dialogue context, which may include the user's beliefs, goals, and intentions as well as the history of the dialogue. Dialogue context information may also be used to rank the hypotheses produced by the ASR and SLU components, taking into account the effects of speech recognition errors.

Dialogue context information in graph-based systems is usually represented implicitly in the states and transitions of the dialogue graph. For example, in Figure 2.1, the system asks a question associated with each state (Destination, Day, etc.) and receives responses that determine the transition to the next state. The information elicited is usually stored in variables to be collected into a database query template and there may be conditional transitions that depend on the user's response, as in the yes/no alternative in the "Destination" confirmation state. If there is a user preference model, it is likely to consist of a small number of elements that determine the dialogue flow. For example, the system could have a mechanism for looking up user information to determine whether the user has previous experience of this system. This information could then be used to allow different paths through the system (e.g., with less verbose instructions), or to address user preferences without having to ask for them.

In frame-based systems, dialogue context information is encoded in the slots of the frames that represent the dialogue task. In addition to a set of attribute–value pairs as used in many frame-based systems as illustrated earlier, more complex data structures can be used. Goddeau et al. (1996) developed a system using E-forms, in which the slots may have different priorities for different users. For example, for some users the color of a car may be more critical than the model or mileage. The E-form is used for dialogue control to determine the system's next response, which is based on the current status of the E-form, the most recent system prompt, and the number of items returned from the database.

Another data structure that has been used to control the dialogue is the schema. Schemas are used in the Carnegie Mellon Communicator system to model more complex tasks than the basic information retrieval tasks that use forms (Constantinides et al., 1998; Rudnicky et al., 1999). A schema is a strategy for dialogue, such as determining an itinerary. The itinerary is represented as a hierarchical data structure that is constructed interactively over the course of the dialogue. At the same time, the nodes in the tree are filled with specific information about the trip. Although there is a default sequence of actions to populate the tree that is maintained as a stack-based agenda, the user and the system can both control this ordering and cause the focus of the dialogue to shift (e.g., Let's talk about the first leg [of the itinerary] again).

In the Queen's Communicator system (McTear el al., 2005), a more complex type of frame, called a DialogFrame, is used to represent information about the current state of the dialogue and to inform dialogue control. A DialogFrame consists of the usual slots contained in a frame, but is supplemented by information concerning the confirmation status of the more recently acquired information from the user, the level to which this information has been confirmed, and the system's intention in respect of the information. For example, the DialogFrame:

[Hilton; NEW FOR SYSTEM; 0; confirm]

indicates that the value "Hilton" has the confirmation status of NEW_FOR_SYSTEM, with a discourse peg of 0, and a system intention to confirm the value.

In general, a Dialogue Context Model may include knowledge sources such as the following:

- *A dialogue history*: A record of the dialogue so far in terms of the propositions that have been discussed and the entities that have been mentioned.
- *A task record*: A representation of the information to be gathered in the dialogue. This record, often referred to as a form, frame, template, or status graph, is used to determine what information has been acquired by the system and what information still has to be acquired.
- *A domain model*: This contains specific information about the domain in question, for example, flight information. Often, this information is encoded in a database from which

relevant information is retrieved by the dialogue system, but in more general cases it could be represented in other ways, for example, in an ontology.

- *A model of conversational competence*: This includes generic knowledge of the principles of conversational turn-taking and discourse obligations—for example, that an appropriate response to a request for information is to supply the information or provide a reason for not supplying it. This information is often encoded in a data structure known as the "agenda."
- *A user preference model*: This model may contain relatively stable information about the user that may be relevant to the dialogue—such as the user's age, gender, and preferences—as well as information that changes over the course of the dialogue, such as the user's goals, beliefs, and intentions.

These knowledge sources are used in different ways and to different degrees according to the dialogue strategy chosen. Examples to be presented in subsequent chapters will illustrate the use of these knowledge sources in more detail.

2.3   DIALOGUE CONTROL AND DIALOGUE MODELING USING VoiceXML

Although a variety of toolkits have been used to implement script and frame-based dialogue, such as the CSLU toolkit (Cole, 1999) and the Philips SpeechMania platform (Aust et al., 1995), these and similar toolkits have been largely superseded by the emergence of VoiceXML toward the end of the 1990s.

VoiceXML is a markup language based on XML that is designed for creating system-directed spoken dialogue systems. VoiceXML was conceived within the Voice BrowserWorking Group of the World Wide Web Consortium (W3C) as a result of various industry initiatives with the aim of providing a standard language that would facilitate code portability and reuse. VoiceXML is a part of the W3C Speech Interface Framework (http://www.w3.org/TR/voice-intro/) and is supplemented by several additional markup languages, including Speech Recognition Grammar Specification (SRGS), Speech Synthesis Markup Language (SSML), Semantic Interpretation for Speech Recognition (SISR), and Call Control Extensible Markup Language (CCXML). A voice platform for implementing spoken dialogue systems using VoiceXML as the dialogue scripting language will contain these components along with the required telephony platform to handle telephone calls to the system and an interface to knowledge sources on a Web server. Figure 2.2 shows the basic components of a VoiceXML application.

The basic element of interaction in VoiceXML is the form. This is analogous to a Web-based form that contains a number of fields to be filled by the user. VoiceXML forms are filled using spoken interaction in which the system prompts for input in one or more fields within the form

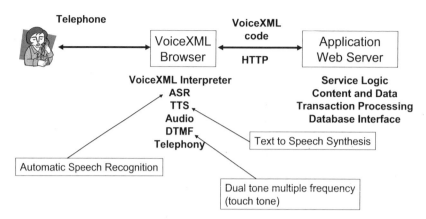

FIGURE 2.2: Components of a VoiceXML application.

and the user responds to the system's prompt. The fields also contain grammars that specify the set of permissible inputs for each field. VoiceXML script is interpreted by a VoiceXML browser. The following is an example of a form containing two fields.

```
<form id = "flight_info">
   <field name = "source">
      <grammar src="airports.grxml" />
      <prompt> Where are you flying from? </prompt>
   </field>
   <field name = "destination">
      <grammar src="airports.grxml" />
      <prompt> Where are you flying to? </prompt>
   </field>
</form>
```

An alternative interactive element is the menu, which presents a number of options to the user. The <menu> element is particularly useful in VoiceXML because it also provides a simple method for specifying the next stage in the dialogue following the user's choice, such as another form or VoiceXML document, as in the following example:

```
<menu id="mainmenu">
   <prompt> Do you want flight arrivals or flight departures? </prompt>
   <choice next="arrivals.vxml"> flight arrivals </choice>
   <choice next="departures.vxml"> flight departures </choice>
</menu>
```

The text within the <choice> element specifies the user's input, whereas the value of the "next" attribute specifies the next transition given that input.

Dialogue control and dialogue modeling are interleaved in VoiceXML. Dialogue control is effected by the FIA, which enables the developer to provide a mainly declarative description of the dialogue by simply specifying the fields of a form, including the prompts and recognition grammars. The processing of the form is controlled by the FIA. Two types of dialogue are possible:

- Directed dialogue
- Mixed-initiative dialogue

In the case of a directed dialogue, the FIA progresses sequentially through each field in a form, executing the prompts and processing the user input. The interpretation of the user input is managed through grammars associated with each prompt. Once the values of the user's responses to the prompts have been elicited within the fields, they are assigned to the field variables. Thus, using the sample code above, if the user says "Belfast" in response to the prompt "Where are you flying from?" with the field called "source," the value "Belfast" is assigned to the field variable "source."

Dialogue control in a mixed-initiative dialogue operates by first prompting for more open-ended input, then once one or more values have been elicited in the response to this prompt, reverting to directed dialogue mode to collect values for the remaining fields. This is accomplished through the FIA, which visits the fields for which values have not yet been defined. Once a field has a defined value, the FIA skips that field. Thus, if certain fields are filled as a result of the user's initial input, then the FIA will only prompt for values in the fields that are still undefined. For example, if the user produces an utterance such as "A flight from Belfast to London departing on Friday." In this case, the values "Belfast," "London," and "Friday" would be extracted from the utterance and assigned respectively to the field variables "Source," "Destination," and "Departure Day." This is achieved by a grammar covering such utterances and augmented with semantic tags that make the appropriate assignments to the field variables.

This mechanism is similar to the frame-based dialogue control discussed in the previous section except that in many frame-based systems the system does not necessarily revert to directed dialogue mode following the first prompt. More generally, it should be noted that the term "mixed-initiative dialogue" is also used to refer to interactions that more closely resemble naturally occurring human conversation in which either dialogue partner can ask questions, change topics, request clarifications, and so on. This type of interaction requires more comprehensive speech and language processing to handle a wider range of user utterances as well as methods for keeping track of the dialogue as it evolves dynamically. Some examples of systems that provide mechanisms for this type of interaction are presented in Chapter 4.

The dialogue context model is achieved in VoiceXML through the use of field variables to which the values of the items extracted from the user's utterance are assigned. Thus, each field is similar to a frame in that it contains a representation of what the user has said, although in the simplest form of a value for a field variable. This information, which constitutes the dialogue context model, is used as described earlier to direct the operations of the FIA and thus determine dialogue control.

2.4 STATISTICAL APPROACHES TO DIALOGUE CONTROL AND DIALOGUE MODELING

Traditionally, dialogue control has been implemented using handcrafted rules created by a dialogue designer on the basis of various design decisions. For example, handling potential ASR misrecognitions might involve considerations of whether and when to confirm the user's input and whether to use information such as ASR confidence scores. These design decisions, which are generally based on experience and best practice guidelines, are applied in an iterative process of design and testing until the optimal system is produced.

What constitutes an optimal spoken dialogue system depends on issues such as the purpose of the system, its intended users, costs involved in usage, such as telephone charges, and so on. Generally, an optimal system is one that completes the transaction successfully and efficiently. Successful completion is measured in terms of whether the user's goal is achieved, for example, to make a flight booking, whereas efficient completion is measured in terms of metrics such as the number of interactions required, the number of confirmations required, and the performance of the speech recognizer. Potentially, the goals of transaction success and transaction efficiency can be in conflict as achieving transaction success may involve a longer dialogue, whereas methods for achieving a shorter dialogue may impede the ultimate success of the transaction—for example, not using confirmations could lead to misunderstandings. To address these issues, designers typically experiment with various choices, such as prompt design, choice of language models for speech recognition, and choice of confirmation strategy.

However, the handcrafted approach requires an expert designer to define the most appropriate rules for each specific dialogue task. A major problem with the approach is that it is difficult, if not impossible, to design all the rules that would be required to cover all potential interactions of a dialogue system, particularly when taking into account the uncertainties that pervade every level of dialogue, from the recognition of what words were spoken to understanding the intentions behind the words.

An alternative is to use data-driven and/or statistical approaches to design dialogue systems and system components, and to optimize decisions of what to do next in the dialogue. Three different approaches can be distinguished: supervised learning, utility maximization, and reinforcement learning (RL). Supervised learning can be used when there is a corpus of dialogues that provide examples of the optimal decisions to take in a dialogue. An example of this approach will be presented in Chapter 3 with reference to error handling. With utility maximization and RL, the idea is to specify priorities for the system in terms of a real-valued objective function; optimization then decides what action to take in a given state in order to maximize the objective function. In utility maximization, the action with the maximum immediate utility is selected (see, e.g., Paek and Horwitz 1999, 2000; see also the discussion of the Conversational Architectures Project in Chapter 4). In RL, the action that maximizes the sum of utilities over time is taken. In the RL literature, these utilities are called "reward" for the immediate gain associated with an action, whereas the sum of reward over time is known as the "return." RL can involve offline optimization, where the system "learns" by conducting dialogues with a simulated user, which itself may be estimated from data, and online optimization, in which a system "learns" by speaking with real users. The following sections illustrate the RL approach to dialogue control in more detail.

2.4.1   Optimizing Dialogue Control Using RL

The key idea in RL is that the priorities of the dialogue system can be specified in a (real-valued) reward function, and that an optimization algorithm is applied to choose actions that maximize that function. In other words, the designer specifies the outcomes (s)he wants and the algorithm works out the details. The optimal policy consists of choosing the best action at each state in the dialogue in order to achieve a given success metric, such as a successful and efficient completion of the dialogue or some measure of user satisfaction.

In the first applications of RL to spoken dialogue systems (e.g., Levin et al., 2000), dialogue was formalized as a Markov Decision Process (MDP) where:

S is a set of system states
$A_{\mathbf{s}}$ is a set of actions that the system can take
T is a set of transition probabilities $P_{\mathrm{T}}(S_t | S_{t-1}, a_{t-1})$, that is, the probability of the next state given the previous one and the previous action
R is an immediate reward that is associated with taking a particular action in a given state

The state space represents the state of the dialogue system at a certain point in time s_t. The set of actions describe what the system can do at s_t, and the policy π, which is a mapping between the state space and the action set, prescribes for any given state what should be the next action to perform. Thus, transition from state s_t to state s_{t+1} is determined by the DM's choice of action a_t at s_t given the user's action and the ASR result. For example, in a flight information system, the DM starts in an initial uninformed state about the values of certain parameters that form the basis of the user's information request—such as the destination, origin, date, and time of the flight. Over the course of the dialogue, the DM elicits values for these parameters and eventually arrives at a state in which it can access a database and offer one or more flights that satisfy the user's requirements. The DM may have a choice of actions at a given state s_t. For example, the DM might ask the user questions about the values of unknown attributes, ask questions to verify known attributes, clarify some misunderstanding, or access a database. To behave optimally, the DM must select an action in each state that has the maximum reward (immediate gain), where the choice of action is based on the information that the DM has available to itself in its current state.

Given such an MDP, learning the best dialogue strategy is a matter of computing an optimal policy π for choosing actions in an MDP that maximizes the expected sum of the rewards received over the transaction (known as the "return"). With multiple action choices at each state, RL is used to explore the choices systematically and to compute the best policy for action selection based on rewards associated with each state transition, using empirical data such as interactions of real or simulated users with the system. Since RL algorithms typically take many hundreds of dialogues to learn an optimal strategy, they will explore other strategies along the way, some of which can be spurious. As a result, learning often starts by using a simulated user since real users would typically not tolerate hundreds of dialogues with nonsensical behavior.

The reward captures the immediate consequences of executing an action in a state. For example, each user interaction may incur a small negative reward, whereas successfully concluding the dialogue may result in a large positive reward. Other rewards may include the number of corrections, the number of accesses to a database, speech recognition errors, dialogue duration, and user satisfaction measures. In some studies (e.g., Walker, 2000), the performance function is a combination of a number of these measures, as in the PARADISE dialogue evaluation methodology (Walker et al., 1997), which combines measures of task efficiency and user satisfaction.

Example: the NJFun system. The NJFun system, which helps people choose recreational activities in New Jersey, is an example of how RL can be applied to decision making in dialogue management using an MDP (Singh et al., 2002). In this system, the relevant dialogue decisions involved choices of dialogue initiative, system prompt, grammar type, and confirmation strategy. The range of initiative when asking or re-asking for an attribute was defined as follows:

- System initiative, which involves a directive prompt and a restrictive grammar
- User initiative, which involves an open prompt and a nonrestrictive grammar
- Mixed initiative, which involves a directive prompt and a nonrestrictive grammar

With system initiative, the user's response is constrained to providing the values requested, so that a restrictive grammar that permits a limited range of utterances can be used. System initiative is a safe strategy that maximizes the likelihood of successful recognition of the input, but at a cost of an inflexible and potentially longer dialogue. User initiative, on the other hand, provides an open prompt with a nonrestrictive grammar (e.g., *how may I help you?*), that permits a wider range of user responses but with a greater potential for recognition of errors requiring subsequent correction. Mixed initiative, as defined in this system, is a compromise between system and open initiative.

As far as confirmations were concerned, the choice was between the use of explicit confirmation or no confirmation. Confirmations are the main mechanism for establishing whether information is grounded. However, explicit confirmation of each item of information may result in a longer dialogue. Thus, the choice of action in terms of dialogue initiative and confirmation strategy has consequences in terms of a number of measures of dialogue performance, such as transaction success, dialogue duration, proportion of turns required for correction, and user satisfaction.

For the purposes of learning a dialogue policy, a dialogue state vector was created consisting of the following variables:

[Greet, attribute, confidence, value, times, grammar, history].

The variable *attribute* keeps track of task-based information, such as the particular attribute value that is currently being elicited or verified. Other variables measure the quality of the dialogue relevant to DM's action choices. For example, *confidence* measures speech recognition confidence for the attribute value in question, *times* measures how often DM has asked about the attribute (a measure of difficulty), whereas *history* measures whether there were difficulties earlier in the dialogue. Thus, these measures of quality provide DM with important information to decide, at each state, whether to adopt a safe as opposed to a more open policy concerning the choice of dialogue initiative and confirmation strategy. Given these attributes and their sets of values, the dialogue state space that

TABLE 2.1: Components of the NJFun dialogue state space.	
ATTRIBUTE	**VALUES**
Greet (G)	0, 1
Attribute being queried (A)[1]	1, 2, 3, 4
Confidence (C)	0, 1, 2, 3, 4
Value of attribute (V) (undefined, known)	0, 1
Times attribute queried (T)	0, 1, 2
Grammar (M) (restrictive, nonrestrictive)	0, 1
Dialogue history (H) (problematic, successful)	0, 1

1, Activity; 2, location; 3, time; 4, date.

S1: Welcome to NJFun. How may I help you?

U1: I'd like to find um winetasting in Lambertville in the morning.

(ASR: I'd like to find out wineries the in the Lambertville in the morning.)

S2: Did you say you are interested in Lambertville?

U2: Yes.

S3: Did you say you want to go in the morning?

U3: Yes.

S4: I found a winery near Lambertville that is open in the morning.

It is the Poor Richard's Winery in Lambertville.

Thank you for using the system.

Please give me feedback by saying `good', `so-so', or `bad'.

U4: Good.

S5: Goodbye and have a nice day!

FIGURE 2.3: An example dialogue with NJFun.

was created to include only those states where DM had an action choice, consisted of 42 possible states with two action choices each, giving a search space of 2^{42} possible dialogue strategies to be explored by RL. Table 2.1 shows the components of the dialogue state space.

Figure 2.3 gives an example of a dialogue generated by the system.

Table 2.2 provides a representation of the dialogue in which each row indicates the state that NJFun is in, the action executed in this state, the corresponding turn in the dialogue, and the reward received. In NJFun, the reward is always 0, except at the final state where the reward takes on the value 1 if NJFun queries the database using exactly the attributes specified in the task description,

TABLE 2.2: Example of a dialogue transaction in the NJFun system.

	STATE G A C V T M H	ACTION	TURN	REWARD
1	0 1 0 0 0 0 0	GreetU	S1	0
2	1 1 2 1 0 0 0	NoConf	–	0
3	1 2 2 1 0 0 1	ExpConf2	S2	0
4	1 3 2 1 0 0 1	ExpConf3	S3	0
5	1 4 0 0 0 0 0	Tell	S4	1

GreetU refers to an open-ended system prompt, such as "Hello—how may I help you?"

and the value −1 otherwise. This measure of task completion is referred to in this study as "binary completion."

The dialogue transaction shown in Table 2.2 can be explained as follows:

1. The system tries to obtain value for attribute 1 by executing GreetU (user initiative).
2. Following the user's response, the system has greeted the user and received a value for attribute 1 with high confidence, using a nonrestrictive grammar and so chooses the NoConf strategy (no confirmation).
3. The system is working on attribute 2, which has a value with high confidence, but there is a history of previous difficulties in the dialogue ($h = 1$). The system chooses ExpConf2 strategy (explicit confirmation of attribute 2).
4. Attribute 3 is acquired in the same manner as attribute 2 and with the same values for ASR and dialogue history.
5. The system consults the database, tells the user the information, and receives a reward.

Experimental dialogues were collected to train and test the system. A version of NJFun was implemented that would choose randomly between two available actions at any state where there was a choice of actions. Given that there were 42 choice states, the total number of policies to explore was 2^{42}. This random exploration of policies exemplifies systems with a nonhandcrafted DM. During both training and testing, the subjects carried out dialogues with the system according to a set of six tasks and after completing the tasks the users filled out a survey and rated the system on a number of subjective measures. The training phase resulted in 311 dialogues in which there was a fairly balanced distribution of action choices at each state. These dialogues were used to construct an empirical MDP in which the reward function was based on the binary measure of task completion discussed earlier. After this, the optimal dialogue policy was computed for this learned MDP.

The learned strategy indicated that an optimal use of initiative is to begin with the more open user initiative and to back off to either system or mixed initiative when required to re-ask for an attribute. Such a strategy makes sense because it provides for an open and potentially short dialogue with a recovery measure if things go wrong. Similarly, the results for confirmation also reflect common sense, with the optimal strategy being to confirm values acquired at lower confidence levels. Other results were more subtle, however. For example, the choice of strategy for reasking was system initiative for the first attribute (activity type) and mixed initiative for the second attribute (activity location). In terms of confirmation, the level of confidence was different across attributes, for example, level 2 (high) for the first attribute, but sometimes lower levels for the other attributes. Other features of the state information affected the confirmation strategy, such as the type of grammar used and the dialogue history.

The optimized policy was experimentally evaluated in the testing phase in which NJFun was reimplemented to use the learned policy. The same tasks that were used in the training phase were performed by 21 test subjects and results for the training and test versions of the systems were compared. The task completion measure that was used to optimize the learned policy increased from 52% in the training dialogues to 64% in the testing dialogues. The performance of the learned policy was also evaluated with respect to some other potential reward measures that had not been used to optimize the test system, such as speech recognition accuracy (ASR), showing a significant improvement from training to testing, even though the learned policy used for testing was not optimized for ASR.

The performance of the learned policy was also compared to some fixed policies that are often recommended in the dialogue systems design literature, including a policy that always uses system initiative and does not confirm, and a policy that always uses user initiative and confirms. It was found that the learned policy performed better than these fixed policies.

The ability to optimize a dialogue policy by searching through a much larger search space than can be explored using handcrafted methods revealed some interesting findings. For example, it was shown how the combination of task-related and dialogue quality-related variables produced interesting strategies suggesting that the system's action choices are determined partly by what is being asked and partly by the system's assessment of the success of the dialogue so far. Some of these choices provide a more fine-grained basis for decision making compared with those investigated in traditional empirical studies.

From MDPs to Partially Observable Markov Decision Processes (POMDPs). One of the main problems with using MDPs to model dialogue is that in an MDP it is assumed that the contents of the system state are fully observable. However, given the various uncertainties inherent in dialogue interactions, it cannot be assumed that the system state is correct. One problem is that the system cannot be certain that it has correctly interpreted the user's intentions (or dialogue act) given the uncertainties associated with speech recognition and SLU. There may also be ambiguities and uncertainties related more generally to the user's goals and intentions, even when speech recognition and spoken language understanding are perfect. For these reasons, a partially observable model of the dialogue is preferred over the standard MDP model. Such a partially observable model of the dialogue process can be represented using a POMDP.

In a POMDP, the model is extended with a system belief state that maintains a probability distribution over dialogue states. In other words, rather than maintaining just one single hypothesis for the current dialogue state, which may be incorrect given the uncertainties mentioned earlier, a set of hypotheses is maintained. Thus, at any given time t, the system is in some unobserved state s_t and has a belief state b, which is a distribution over possible states. Given b, an action a is selected, a reward r is received, and the system moves to another unobserved state s_{t+1}. Maintaining and updating b is referred to as belief monitoring. For further details of the application of the POMDP model to spoken dialogue systems, see Williams and Young (2007a).

The use of POMDPs also provides a principled method for dealing with the uncertainties associated with the ASR and SLU components. Whereas in an MDP the output from these components is treated as a single interpretation, usually in the form of the dialogue act that the system assumes that the user has intended with their utterance, in a POMDP the *n*-best lists from ASR and SLU can be maintained as multiple hypotheses. This enables the system to proceed even if confidence in the ASR/SLU is low. The user model provides a probability of each user act given each possible dialogue hypothesis and if a misunderstanding is detected, the system does not necessarily need to backtrack. Each time a new observation is received, such as a new user input, the belief distribution is recalculated.

2.4.2 Applying POMDPs to Dialogue Systems: An Example

The application of POMDPs as statistical models for spoken dialogue systems is problematic, due to factors such as the large space of possible belief states. To address this issue, Williams and Young (2007b) developed an online method for policy optimization called summarized Q-learning that was subsequently applied in a study involving a tourist information system with real users (Thomson et al., 2007). In this study, rewards were based on task completion (positive reward) and the number of dialogue turns (negative reward). The system was trained and the policy score converged after approximately 25,000 dialogues. Next, the system was tested with real users and performance was measured based on whether the system's recommendation matched all the constraints specified for the task, with 90.6% of the dialogues meeting this criterion. In another study, Williams and Young (2007a) presented empirical results from simulation experiments in which a POMDP-based dialogue system was compared with a handcrafted system. One result from this study showed how the POMDP system outperformed the handcrafted system in terms of error handling, which was due to its ability to maintain multiple hypotheses for each slot as compared to the handcrafted system, which could only maintain one hypothesis and had to discard the others.

Although in these systems the task for the spoken dialogue system involved slot-filling, in a study by Williams (2007) a troubleshooting system is presented that advises users how to fix malfunctioning equipment. This is a more challenging domain as, in addition to problems involving uncertainties of user input and user beliefs, the system also has to deal with uncertainties about whether the user has misinterpreted some output from the equipment, such as the meaning or color of a light, or has performed some erroneous action, such as pressing the wrong button. Thus, in this domain the system cannot know the true state of the product nor of the user's actions. A state-based handcrafted DM was created as a baseline, consisting of 19 dialogue states with a specified action to be taken in each state and specified transitions based on transitions from the speech recognizer or from troubleshooting tests. This system was then compared with a POMDP-based system, using 500 simulated dialogues for each system. The results showed that in the presence of speech recognition errors, the POMDP produced shorter and more successful dialogues, and that it also performed better when the handcrafted system was run without speech recognition errors. Table 2.3 (from Williams, 2007, p. 8) presents an extract from a dialogue with the POMDP DM that illustrates how the POMDP DM can progress the dialogue despite low confidence and nonsensical user input by making use of its belief state.

In Table 2.3, asterisks (*) indicate transitions not in the baseline handcrafted dialogue manager. $p_{(allOk)}$ shows the probability that DSL connectivity is working and $p_{(pwrOn)}$ shows the probability that the power to the DSL modem is on, according to the POMDP belief state. The simulated user's communicative actions are shown in italics, followed by the [concept, confidence score] produced by the ASR simulation.

As an example of the different strategies that would be taken by different systems, at **U4** and **U8** the handcrafted system would have ignored the low confidence recognitions whereas the POMDP policy is able to move ahead. When a nonsensical input is received, as in **U6**, the POMDP system is able to revert back to an earlier stage of troubleshooting that it had previously skipped, thus enabling it to accomplish the task faster without sacrificing task completion.

2.4.3   Some Issues in the Application of RL to Dialogue Management

A crucial issue in RL concerns the tractability of large state–action spaces. For this reason, many early approaches have used small state spaces and action sets. Thus, although in principle an MDP state could include any possible information about the dialogue, in practice it was often restricted, as in the NJFUN system (Singh et al., 2002) to a more limited set of items, such as:

- The values of the slots in the current frame —for example, values for slots such as "destination" and "origin" in a flight booking system
- The most recent question asked by the system
- The user's most recent answer
- ASR confidence

Given these restrictions, it is important to design the state space such that it is sufficiently rich to support the learning of an accurate model while minimizing data sparseness. Similar problems apply to POMDPs. One solution being developed is the Hidden Information State model, in which the state space is partitioned so that partition beliefs are computed instead of state beliefs and the master state space is reduced into a summary space (Williams and Young, 2007a, 2007b). The Hidden Information State addresses the dialogue modeling problem of how to track multiple hypotheses efficiently; the "summary space" addresses the *dialogue management* problem of how to keep learning the optimal DM tractable. Other approaches to the issue of tractability include Linear

ID	$P_{(allOk)}$	$P_{(pwrOn)}$	TRANSCRIPT
*S1	56%	98.0%	I'm going to try pinging your DSL modem from here.
S2	–	–	There was no response so it seems that your connection isn't working yet.
*S3	14%	96.1%	Please turn the DSL modem on.
U4	–	–	*ok* [ok, 0.004]
*S5	30%	96.4%	What color is the network light on the DSL modem?
U6	–	–	*dontunderstand* [ok, 0.452]
*S7	30%	93.8%	Please turn the DSL modem on.
U8	–	–	*dontunderstand* [ok, 0.454]
*S9	31%	99.1%	I'm going to check if there are any outages reported, just a moment.
S10	–	–	There are no outages reported.
S11	39%	99.1%	I'm going to try resetting your connection from here, just a moment.
S12	–	–	Ok, that has been done.
S13	48%	99.1%	What color is the network light on the DSL modem?
U14	–	–	*red* [red, 0.678]
S15	3%	99.8%	Please open the DSL configuration screen.
. . .	. . .	. . .	. . .

TABLE 2.3: Fragment of a conversation with the POMDP dialogue manager.

From Williams (2007).

Function Approximation (Henderson et al., 2005) and Hierarchical RL (Lemon et al., 2006). By using these methods, it has been possible to use more complex state representations and to learn policies for larger sets of dialogue actions (Lemon and Pietquin, 2007).

Another factor is the amount of data that is required for training and testing. Using real users quickly becomes impractical as tens of thousands of dialogues may be required for training more complex systems. For this reason, dialogue (or user) simulators are increasingly being used to simulate dialogues with the system (see Schatzmann et al., 2006, for a review of the use of dialogue simulators in RL).

Comparing the performance of RL-based dialogue management strategies with those using handcrafted rules is difficult because it assumes that the handcrafted strategies in the baseline system remain static, whereas in reality they are refined as part of the iterative process of dialogue systems development. For example, in the fragment presented in Table 4.4, it was observed that the baseline handcrafted system ignored the low confidence recognitions whereas the POMDP DM was able to take these into account. However, it would be possible to add new rules to the handcrafted system to address this deficiency. In other words, what is required is a more comprehensive comparison that evaluates the performance of a more extensively developed handcrafted system and also takes into account factors such as the effort required to continually refine such a system compared with the effort required to learn an optimal strategy using the POMDP approach.

Finally, regarding the practical deployment of RL for dialogue systems development, there are a number of issues that need to be addressed (Paek, 2007). The objective function that determines the optimal dialogue policy is generally based on maximization of the expected cumulative reward or on posthoc measures of usability. However, it is not clear whether every dialogue should be seen in terms of such an optimization problem. Moreover, it is likely that most developers would not have the required experience with optimization to choose or adapt an objective function. The local reward, which contributes to the expected cumulative reward, is also problematic. The normal procedure is to penalize the system for additional turns in the interests of dialogue efficiency; yet, in some dialogues where the user wishes to explore different possibilities, it may be preferable to increase the reward for longer dialogues. A third problem concerns the policy that is learned by a DM using RL, as the reasons for the decisions taken by the DM are unlikely to be clear to users or system designers. Given the commercial need to satisfy customers and to be able to fix design problems, designers will wish to keep more control over the design of their systems and, in any case, are unlikely to be able to remedy problems of learned dialogue policies without a deep knowledge of RL (Williams, 2008). Recent work on this topic has integrated the conventional manual design that incorporates business rules and design knowledge with POMDPs to produce more efficient systems in which the conventional DM nominates a set of one or more actions and the POMDP DM chooses the optimal one (Williams, 2008). Using this method, spurious action choices that would have been explored by the POMDP DM are pruned so that optimization can run faster and more reliably than in a POMDP system that did not take account of such designer knowledge.

In summary, RL offers a promising and principled mathematical framework for handling uncertainty in spoken dialogue systems and supports the design of the dialogue management component by enabling the DM to learn an optimal dialogue policy. Recent results have demonstrated superior performance of RL systems compared to handcrafted baseline systems and there is some evidence that POMDPs can be scaled to handle real-world tasks. There are still many challenges facing the application of RL to spoken dialogue systems, both in terms of issues of tractability and availability of training data as well as in terms of practical deployment.

2.5   SUMMARY

This chapter has reviewed the processes of dialogue management in terms of dialogue control and dialogue context modeling. In the first part of the chapter, the most widely used methods for dialogue management involving graphs and frames were described, followed by an overview of VoiceXML, which makes use of both methods. Most commercial work has made use of the graph- and frame-based approaches. Their main advantages are that they are simple to develop and maintain, and they do not necessarily require advanced representations or processing. Moreover, the interactions that they support are effective in that they provide an intuitive interface for the user that facilitates the successful achievement of simple transactions.

Statistical and data-driven approaches to dialogue management offer an alternative to traditional handcrafted and rule-based methods. RL, in which dialogue is modeled in terms of actions and states using either the MDP or POMDP approaches, enables the automatic optimization of dialogue decisions as well as a more principled way of handling uncertainty.

Given the inherent uncertainty in the dialogue process, it is important to consider methods to support robustness. In addition to the use of POMDPs for this purpose, considerable effort has also been devoted to the issue of error handling. This is the subject of the next chapter. Then Chapter 4 will present a number of frameworks and case studies that build on and extend the approaches to dialogue management presented in this chapter.

CHAPTER 3

Error Handling

Miscommunication can occur in any communicative interaction, so it is important that a spoken dialogue system should have mechanisms for detecting and dealing with errors given the impact that errors can have on dialogue performance. For example, in one study it was found that when the frequency of error was low, the impact on task success was minor, but when error rates increased, the expected chance of task success dropped considerably (Bohus and Rudnicky, 2008).

Error handling is an active research topic within spoken dialogue technology (as is evidenced, e.g., by recent collections of articles in Carlson et al., 2005, and Dybkjær and Minker, 2008), and also by recent dissertations on error handling by Bohus (2007) and Skantze (2007). To date, most work has focused on errors caused by inaccurate speech recognition since the majority of errors tend to occur at this level (Bohus and Rudnicky, 2008). The following example (from Bohus, 2007, p. 23) illustrates some speech recognition errors that occurred in a spoken language dialogue between a human user and an automated system (the system's interpretation of the user's input is in brackets and upper case):

S1: What city are you leaving from?
U1: Urbana Champaign [OKAY IN THAT SAME PAY]
S2: Sorry I'm not sure I understood what you said. What city are you leaving from?
U2: Urbana Champaign [FOR MINUTE SINCE HEY]
S3: I'm still having trouble understanding you. To go on, I need you to answer the following question. What city are you leaving from?
U3: Chicago [CHICAGO]
S4: Traveling from Chicago. Where would you like to go?
U4: Huntsville [SEOUL]
S5: Traveling to Seoul. What day did you need to travel?
U5: No, no, I'm traveling to Birmingham [THE TRAVELING TO BERLIN PM]
S6: Traveling in the afternoon. Okay what day would you be departing Chicago?
U6: Uh, the tenth of august [AT THE TENTH OF AUGUST]

S7: A flight tomorrow I have a Korean Airlines flight departing Chicago at 1:40 P.M., arrives Seoul at 5 P.M. the next day. Do you want to take that?

U7: My destination is Birmingham [FLIGHT DESTINATION MR WEEKEND]

S8: Traveling on Saturday, August 12th—I have a flight departing Chicago at 1:40 P.M. arrives Seoul at. . .

As can be seen from this example, the system (**S**) is unable to correctly recognize the user's (**U**) spoken input for the departure and arrival cities, and also makes errors with the time and date.

One way to handle errors is to try to prevent their occurrence through careful design of prompts, recognition grammars, dialogue flows, and verification strategies (Cohen et al., 2004). Prompts are designed so that they make clear to the user what they can say, and grammars are constructed that can recognize the predicted user input. Further constraints are imposed by designing a system-directed dialogue, so that the user's options are restricted to responding to the system's prompts, whereas verifications are used to check that the system has correctly recognized the user's utterances.

However, these methods are not sufficient given the current state of speech recognition technology, since it cannot be guaranteed that the system has correctly recognized what the user actually said, making it essential for the system to be able to detect when an error has occurred and to be able to take an appropriate action to deal with it. In the simplest case, error handling is predetermined at design time using fairly simple techniques for error detection and repair. For example, if the confidence score for an utterance is lower than a preset threshold, the utterance will be rejected and the user may be asked to repeat or rephrase the input. Subsequent failures to understand may be handled by providing more help on the next occasion and eventually transferring the call to a human operator.

More complex methods in which the system takes decisions dynamically based on a variety of factors such as the current state of the dialogue and the costs and benefits of repairing an error have also been developed. These approaches are based on the theory of grounding, which states that participants in a dialogue collaborate to establish common ground—that is, the mutual belief that their dialogue utterances and obligations have been understood (Clark, 1996; Traum, 1999). In this view, error handling involves deciding what to do when an error is detected (or suspected). Generally, this involves following the principle of least effort in seeking to minimize the costs of grounding. Thus, while ensuring that all relevant information has been confirmed, an efficient dialogue manager is also motivated to avoid unnecessary grounding in the interests of shorter and more satisfying transactions. The next section describes basic approaches to error handling in spoken dialogue, followed by some examples of more advanced strategies.

3.1   APPROACHES TO ERROR HANDLING IN SPOKEN DIALOGUE

There are several basic strategies that a system can adopt when faced with a potential error. On one hand, it can simply accept the utterance and continue with the dialogue, as happens in the example above at **U4–S5**. However, with this strategy there is the danger of false acceptance, where the system makes an erroneous interpretation of what the user actually said. This situation is often referred to as a misunderstanding. Misunderstandings are difficult to rectify and in this example the system persists with "Seoul" as the destination city despite the user's attempt to correct this at **U5**.

A second strategy is to reject the utterance and ask the user to repeat or rephrase. An example occurs in lines **S1–S3**, where the system is unable to derive a suitable interpretation of the user's input. This situation is referred to as a nonunderstanding. Detection of this type of error is usually based on the acoustic confidence scores of the user's input when they fall below a given threshold.

A third strategy is to accept the utterance but attempt to verify it, either explicitly or implicitly. An explicit verification would take a form such as "did you say Chicago?" where the user has to answer either "yes" or "no" to verify the system's interpretation. In this example, the system adopts an "implicit verification" strategy, incorporating its interpretation of the user's input in its next question (**S4, S5, S6**). This strategy is less costly in terms of transaction time and user frustration compared with the "explicit confirmation" strategy but has the disadvantage of making error recovery more difficult, as this example illustrates throughout.

Error handling can be viewed in terms of the following processes:

1. *Error detection* involves monitoring the dialogue for cues that some error has occurred.
2. *Error prediction* is concerned with online prediction of potential problems based on evidence from the dialogue so far, such as the performance of the speech recognizer or the number of corrective subdialogues.
3. *Error recovery* involves strategies for putting the dialogue back on track once an error has been detected.

3.1.1   Error Detection

Error detection involves looking for cues that an error has occurred. This can occur when the system detects that there may be an error in the user's current utterance (early detection) or it may be detection later in the dialogue (late detection). As mentioned above, early error detection is usually based on the acoustic confidence scores of the user's input where an error is suspected if the confidence score falls below a predetermined threshold (Komatani and Kawahara, 2000; Hazen et al., 2000). However, this measure is not entirely reliable because there is no one-to-one correspondence between low confidence scores and errors, nor between high confidence scores and correct recognition (Bouwman et al., 1999). Other approaches include:

- Using secondary properties of the decoding process, such as language model backoff patterns and information in the word-hypothesis lattice (Wessel et al., 1998; Evermann and Woodland, 2000).
- Comparison of prosodic cues in correctly and incorrectly recognized utterances to predict speech recognition performance (Litman et al., 2000).
- The use of combinations of cues such as parsing confidence, degree of context shift, and salience to reliably predict errors (Walker et al., 2000b).
- The use of concept confidence scores derived from speech recognition confidence scores using a discourse model of what has been said in the dialogue and what entities have been referred to (Skantze, 2008).

In late error detection, errors are identified based on evidence from the subsequent dialogue that suggests that an error has occurred. Usually, late error detection involves analysis of the user's response to a system verification, using as evidence various positive and negative cues in the user's utterance (Krahmer et al., 2001). Examples of positive cues indicating that the user accepts the system's verification are short turns, unmarked word order, and confirmations, whereas negative cues suggesting a problem include longer turns, marked word order, disconfirmations, and corrections. The following is an example of a user correcting a system that uses implicit verification (in **S2** and **S3**).

> **S1**: Good morning, this is the talking computer. From which station to which station do you wish to travel?
>
> **U1**: From Eindhoven to Reuver.
>
> **S2**: On what day do you want to travel from Eindhoven to Winsum?
>
> **U2**: I want to travel at 8 o'clock from Eindhoven to **Reuver**.
>
> **S3**: On what day do you want to travel from Eindhoven to Utrecht CS at 8 o'clock in the morning?
>
> **U3**: **No, in the evening, at 8 o'clock**. I want to travel from Eindhoven to **Reuver**.

This example illustrates the difficulties that users experience when correcting several values within the same utterance. As far as negative cues are concerned, prosodic information such as extra emphasis on "Reuver," cue words such as "no," and the marked word order in **U3** would identify the possibility of the occurrence of errors.

Krahmer et al. (2001) also investigated whether it would be possible to automatically decide whether a preceding system utterance contained an error. They conducted machine learning experiments using features in the system's verification utterance as well as the positive and negative cues in the user's response and found that the best results (almost 97% accuracy) were obtained when all the features were used in combination. In a companion study, they examined prosodic information in the user's utterance, finding that user utterances that corrected a system verification often contained a high boundary tone, high pitch, as well as a relatively long delay between the end of the system's question and the beginning of the user's answer (Krahmer et al., 2002).

3.1.2   Error Prediction

Error prediction is concerned with the online prediction of potential problems in a dialogue based on features monitored in the dialogue so far. If errors are predicted, then steps can be taken to prevent those errors, for example, by changing the dialogue strategy. Litman et al. (1999) applied machine learning techniques to develop a classifier that could predict dialogues with poor speech recognition performance, using features such as confidence scores as well as measures of dialogue efficiency and quality. The features were collected over the complete dialogue so that it was not possible for the rules learned by the classifier to influence the course of the ongoing dialogue. However, in another study, Walker et al. (2000a) showed how information gathered early in the dialogue could be used to modify the current dialogue strategy. Predictions were based on speech recognition features (confidence scores, utterance duration, and number of recognized words), natural language understanding features (parsing confidence and context shift), and dialogue features (prompts and confirmations). The results showed that rules could be learned to predict problematic dialogues, with accuracy rates ranging from 72% to 87% depending on how much of the dialogue had been seen so far.

3.1.3   Error Recovery

Error recovery can involve a number of different strategies, including asking the user to repeat or rephrase a problematic utterance or using different verification techniques based on the acoustic confidence scores (Sturm et al., 1999). Krahmer et al. (2001) proposed the use of information available in the detection of the error, such as the negative cues in late error detection, to enable the system to construct a more useful follow-up question. Another approach involves the system automatically adapting its dialogue strategies on encountering problems within the dialogue. For example, Litman and Pan (2002) developed a system that reverted to a more conservative dialogue initiative strategy if the dialogue model indicated that misrecognitions had exceeded a given threshold. The following commented example illustrates this type of adaptation (ASR results and scores are again in brackets and upper case).

S1: How may I help you?

(System begins with open-ended question)

U1: I need to find a train going to New York City [DC I DON'T CARE ON THURSDAY. -5.293949]

S2: Which city do you want to leave from?

(Initial setting is "no confirmation." System asks the next question despite the misrecognition—score exceeds threshold of −4)

U2: Baltimore.

S3: Do you want me to find the trains from Baltimore to DC on Thursday at anytime now?

U3: No. I need to leave on Sunday. [DC BETWEEN 1 NIGHT AND 8. -4.916628]

S4: I heard you say go to DC between 1 night and 8. Do you want me to find you the trains from Baltimore to DC on Thursday between 1 night and now?

(System adapts its strategy: there has been at least one misrecognition within the previous four utterances. System uses implicit confirmation "I heard you say. . . ." combined with mixed initiative)

As the comments indicate, the type of confirmation is associated with the ASR scores and information from the dialogue history. For example, if there had been at least one misrecognition within the previous four utterances, the system adapts its dialogue strategy to use system-initiated questions and implicit confirmation. Many spoken dialogue systems make use of confidence scores to determine whether and how to perform grounding. The following is an example of how confidence scores may be associated with grounding actions.

Confidence level	Action
High	Accept
Fairly high	Display understanding (implicit verification)
Fairly low	Clarification request (explicit verification)
Low	Reject

3.2   SOME NEW APPROACHES TO ERROR HANDLING

Recently, a number of approaches to error handling have been developed that involve more advanced approaches to grounding decisions. These approaches use a wider range of information and more principled methods for deciding which strategy to adopt in a particular dialogue context, and they are characterized by data-driven methods as opposed to the mainly rule-based methods that have been discussed in the previous section. This section presents examples of some recent work on error handling for spoken dialogue, including data-driven approaches.

3.2.1   Error Handling Based on the Strategies Used by Humans in Dialogue Strategies

The Higgins spoken dialogue system deals with pedestrian navigation and guidance. The user tells the system where she wants to go and the system provides verbal instructions. As the system does not have access to the user's position, it engages in dialogue about the user's surroundings and dynamically updates its model of the user's position. The error handling strategies in Higgins were developed by Skantze (2007), who investigated, among other things, human error handling strategies when faced with errors of nonunderstanding, error-handling involving concepts as opposed to complete utterances, and a data-driven approach to decisions involving grounding.

The study of human error handling strategies indicated that the strategy commonly used in spoken dialogue systems to signal nonunderstanding often led to error spirals: the user would either repeat the utterance, which is likely to be misunderstood again, or hyper-articulate, which is more likely not to be understood either, since the performance of the ASR worsens if it is not trained on models of hyper-articulated speech (Skantze 2005). It was also found that, despite a high frequency of nonunderstandings in human interactions, the operators giving the instructions tended not to signal nonunderstanding, and, if they did, this had a negative effect on the user's experience of task success. The more usual strategy was to ask a task-related question as in the example below. This led to fewer nonunderstandings of the subsequent user utterance and resulted in a faster recovery from the problem.

> **S1**: Do you see a wooden house in front of you?
> **U1**: I pass the wooden house now [YES CROSSING ADDRESS NOW]: Nonunderstanding
> **S2**: Can you see a restaurant sign?

Error handling in most spoken dialogue systems is based on confidence scores associated with the recognition of complete utterances. In this research, however, grounding status was modeled on the concept level, since it was found that often part of the ASR recognition of an utterance is correct and only a particular concept needs to be repaired. The discourse modeling component kept track of the grounding status of concepts to enable the action managers to select between different types of concept-level error handling strategies such as a clarification request (explicit verification), display of understanding (implicit verification), or a misunderstanding repair. One particular subcategory of clarification request supported by this concept-based modeling was fragmentary clarification, which allowed the user to correct the system when a particular concept had a low grounding status, as for example in the following where 'blue' has a low confidence score:

> **U1**: I can see a blue building
> **S1**: Blue

U2: No
U3: Brown

One of the main innovations in this research was the development of a data-driven approach to decisions involving grounding in spoken dialogue systems. Three sources of information were involved in the grounding decision:

- The confidence scores associated with the user's utterance
- Task consequences—the costs of taking a grounding action
- Task-related costs of rejections and misunderstandings

Confidence scores have often been associated with grounding decisions in spoken dialogue systems, as discussed earlier. However, whereas generally these decisions have been based on handcrafted confidence thresholds, in this study the decisions were learned from data and were combined with the additional factors of task consequences and task-related costs.

Task consequences measure the cost of false acceptance (misunderstanding) versus the cost of false rejection (nonunderstanding). In previous work (e.g., Bohus and Rudnicky, 2001), it was found that false acceptances were more costly than false rejections.

Task-related costs are concerned with the costs of making a rejection or misunderstanding in relation to the current task. In previous work, Paek and Horwitz (1999, 2000) used the principle of maximum expected utility to estimate these costs, where the utilities were directly estimated by the dialogue designer. In Skantze's study, on the other hand, the utilities were estimated from data using a principle of minimum expected cost, where cost was a negative utility. The aim was to find a strategy that would minimize the costs, that is, the sum of all task-related and grounding costs, which were defined by analyzing the consequences of different grounding actions using parameters estimated from data. The cost measure was efficiency, measured in terms of the number of syllables used to complete a repair sequence, and the consequences of different actions given the correctness of recognition hypothesis, which were defined in terms of cost functions, such as:

Cost(ACCEPT, correct)—no cost
Cost(ACCEPT, incorrect)—leads to a misunderstanding and could slow down the dialogue as either system or user will have to repair the error

An additional measure used to estimate costs was Information Gain. For example, some concepts have a high information gain in relation to the task, so these should be clarified. On the other hand, concepts with low information gain can be accepted or rejected, as there is no significant effect on the current task, whereas accepting a concept with a high cost of misunderstanding would require very high confidence in the concept.

3.2.2   Error Handling in the RavenClaw System

RavenClaw is a dialogue management framework developed at Carnegie-Mellon University and used to build and deploy a range of spoken dialogue systems. It was used as an experimental platform for a large-scale empirical investigation that focused in particular on novel methods for error detection, the development and evaluation of a large set of error recovery strategies, and a novel online learning-based approach to developing error recovery policies (Bohus, 2007).

Error detection. Nonunderstanding errors, where the system is unable to obtain an interpretation for a user's utterance, are generally easy to detect using confidence scores. However, given that confidence scores are not necessarily accurate, a problem arises when the system falsely rejects an utterance because of a low confidence score. Raising the rejection threshold can address this problem but at the risk of causing more false acceptances (misunderstandings), which are more difficult to detect and repair. Confidence threshold adjustment is usually based on rules of thumb. Bohus (2007) proposes a data-driven method for optimizing confidence thresholds that involves assessing the costs of errors by relating their frequency to global dialogue performance. The experimental results indicated that different rejection thresholds should be used at different points in the dialogue. For example, it was found that longer user utterances that occurred after the initial prompt ("How may I help you?") were frequently rejected even though they were correctly recognized. Changing the rejection threshold for this dialogue state could be expected to result in an average increase of 0.35% correctly transferred concepts at the expense of a 0.15% increase in incorrectly transferred concepts.

Misunderstandings, where the system obtains an incorrect interpretation of the user's utterance, are also detected using confidence scores. Models for confidence annotation have been developed using supervised learning techniques in which a set of features characterizing the current recognition result and the current context is used to predict whether the user's utterances was correctly interpreted by the system. However, this method requires extensive collection and labeling of data. Bohus (2007) introduced a technique known as an "implicitly supervised learning paradigm," in which the labels are automatically learned from dialogues with users. More specifically, when the system attempts to verify its interpretation of a user's utterance, the system can learn from the user's response whether it had classified the utterance correctly and make adjustments to its confidence annotation model. The following example (from Bohus, 2007: 148) illustrates this method, where R indicates the recognition result and P its semantic representation.

S1: Where are you leaving from?

U1: the airport

      R: LIBERTY and WOOD

      P: [departure=LIBERTY and WOOD]

S2: Leaving from Liberty and Wood. Is that correct?

U2: nope

      R: NO

      P: [NO]

The user's utterance (**U1**) is misrecognized. When the system attempts to verify its interpretation in **S2**, the user rejects this interpretation in **U2**. This information from the user provides useful information that can help the system train or refine its confidence annotation model. In a series of empirical investigations, it was found that the new implicitly supervised learning method attained 80% of the performance of a traditional, fully supervised model, with the advantage of not requiring a labeled corpus for the learning process.

As Bohus suggests, one way to use implicitly supervised learning would be to have the system begin by explicitly confirming all of the information elicited from users. Then, as the system collects more data in the form of labels classifying its interpretation of the user input as correct or incorrect, the system could update its confidence annotation model and only use explicit confirmation when the confidence scores, which would gradually become more reliable, were very low.

The process of updating or changing the confidence model can also be seen as a process of belief updating. In most systems, this is a simple process. For example, if the user responds positively to the system's confirmation attempt, the confidence can be set to high, whereas if the response is negative the confidence can be set to low. Ideally, however, this belief updating process should involve a more extended monitoring of the dialogue in which evidence is integrated across multiple turns. Bohus (2007) developed a solution to this challenge using supervised learning and shows that this approach constructs more accurate beliefs than other approaches based on ad hoc heuristics, with a considerable gain in dialogue effectiveness and efficiency. One interesting aspect of this approach is the tracking and updating of multiple recognition hypotheses using a compressed representation of beliefs in which only the topmost hypotheses are stored, in order to make the learning tractable.

Error recovery. As far as recovery strategies were concerned, 10 different strategies were investigated for recovery following a nonunderstanding by the system of the user's utterance. These included the more obvious strategies used in many spoken dialogue systems of asking the user to repeat or rephrase, and providing various levels of help. It was found that the three most successful strategies were:

1. MoveOn, where the system advances the task by moving on to a different question
2. Help, where a help message is provided that explains the current state of the dialogue and indicates what the user can say
3. TerseYouCanSay, where the system states briefly what the user can say at the current point in the dialogue

These findings are similar to those of Skantze (2005), suggesting that some of the more traditional methods for error recovery, such as asking the user to repeat, are less likely to be successful since once a nonunderstanding error has occurred, there is a good chance that another error will occur if the utterance is repeated. The MoveOn strategy, which was also used by the human operators in Skantze's study, overcomes this problem by moving on to a different question. However, this strategy would only be useful where an alternative question can be used to address the system's dialogue goals.

Given the large number of recovery strategies for nonunderstanding errors, it is important to have good policies for applying the most appropriate strategy. Bohus (2007) developed an online learning-based approach consisting of two steps. First, runtime estimates were constructed for the likelihood of success for each strategy, then a policy was constructed online using these estimates. Some experimental results showed that this approach led to statistically significant improvements in the average nonunderstanding recovery rate.

3.2.3 Error Handling in the DIHANA Project—A Corpus-Based Approach

Torres et al. (2005) present a corpus-based approach to error handling in which the dialogue model is a bigram model as opposed to the complete dialogue history used in the approach of Griol et al. (2006) and Hurtado et al. (2006). For each user or system dialogue act, this model specifies a set of possible transitions to the next dialogue act based on the probabilities of those transitions in the corpus. A set of rules is used along with confidence scores to prevent dialogue inconsistencies. For example, a rule might specify that if an attribute has high confidence, then it does not need to be confirmed, but if it has low confidence, then it should be confirmed. For example, following a user request such as:

To Bilbao on March the second. When does it leave and arrive? And how much is it?
some possible transitions to system states are as follows:

Confirm Destination
Confirm Departure-Date
Give Departure-Hour
Give Arrival-Hour
Give Price

The selection of the most appropriate transition determines the system's dialogue strategy. In this example, if confidence scores are used, and assuming high scores for destination and date but a low score for price, the selected transition and the corresponding system response would be:

(**U**:Question: Depart_hour, Arrival_hour) → (**S**:Answer:Depart_hour, Arrival_hour)
It leaves at six o'clock and arrives at eight o'clock.

In this example, the system provides values for departure and arrival, but it does not confirm the values for destination and date since they have high confidence scores, and it ignores the question about price because of its low confidence score.

The selection of the best transition that will determine the next system act depends on the current system state, the set of possible transitions from that state, and the values obtained in the dialogue so far. In the simplest case, selection of a transition would involve matching the dialogue acts in the user input with the same set of user dialogue acts in the corpus and then selecting the appropriate transition. However, in reality, the situation is more complex. Data sparseness can result in a failure to find an exact match between the user input and the user acts represented in the corpus. There is also the problem of unseen situations, where the user's input does not have a corresponding match in the corpus. Finally, alternative transitions require some method to select the best transition from the set of possible transitions at a given state.

One method to address the issue of finding an association between a user input frame and a similar dialogue act in the corpus is to adapt the user input frame with a function that produces a set of alternative strings that cover some of the content in the original input and provide a match with frames in the corpus. This process is called semantic generalization. The following example illustrates two of the five different methods involved in this process (based on Torres et al., 2005).

Given a user turn consisting of three input frames with confidence scores for the syntactic and semantic analyses in parentheses:

(AFFIRMATION) * [0.78, 0.83]
DESTINATION: Bilbao * [0.82, 0.85]
TRAIN-TYPE: Talgo * [0.62, 0.66]
(DEPART-HOUR) * [0.91, 0.95]
(PRICE) * [0.55, 0.46]

a frame consisting of the following dialogue acts is produced:

(**U**:Affirmation:Destination, Train_type)
(**U**:Question:Depart_hour)
(**U**:Question:Price)

Using semantic generalization, the following alternative frames are produced for this input:

3 (**U**:Question:Depart_hour) (**U**:Question:Price)
4 (**U**:Affirmation:Destination,Train_type) (**U**:Question:Depart_hour)
5 (**U**:Question:Depart_hour, Price)
6 (**U**:Affirmation:Train_type) (**U**:Question:Price)
7 (**U**:Affirmation:Destination) (**U**:Question:Depart_hour)

The first frame is produced using a method based on the principle of recency (unconditional concatenation). In this method, the oldest frames are pruned, on the assumption that earlier items are less important in the input than later items. In this example, the first dialogue act is pruned and the last two dialogue acts are retained. By comparison, the second frame is produced using a method (confidence-conditional concatenation) that takes into consideration the confidence scores associated with the dialogue acts that are placed in a list in ascending order of confidence score, with the frame with the lowest score being discarded. In this case, the frame with the lowest confidence (**U**: Question:Price) is discarded. For details on the remaining three methods of semantic generalization, see Torres et al. (2005). Thus, by producing variant frames that are similar to the original user input in terms of retaining some of the dialogue acts in the input frame, the chances of finding a match with a frame in the corpus are increased.

Once a set of possible transitions has been constructed given the user input, the next task is to choose the best transition. Two processes are involved: pruning irrelevant transitions and adjusting the weights of transitions. Pruning irrelevant transitions takes into account information from previous turns concerning values that have already been elicited or confirmed, as recorded in the dialogue history, such that transitions involving these values are pruned. Adjusting the weights of transitions involves combining the probabilities given by the dialogue manager with the confidence scores given by the Dialogue Register (DR). For example, transitions to confirm attributes with fairly high confidence scores (although not high enough to be pruned) can be weakened, whereas other transitions to confirm attributes with low confidence scores can be strengthened. Likewise, transitions to answer user queries can be weakened or strengthened depending on the confidence scores of the attributes that triggered the query.

The following examples (based on Torres et al., 2005) illustrate how the use of these methods results in different dialogue strategies in terms of which values to confirm. In the first example, all three attributes have high confidence scores, so no confirmation is given:

U0: Hello, I want to go from Burgos to Bilbao on March the second
U0: (DEPART-HOUR) * [0.97, 0.92]
ORIGIN: Burgos * [0.97, 0.92]

      DESTINATION: Bilbao * [0.97, 0.92]

      DEPART-DATE: 02-03-2004 * [0.87, 0.92]

S0: The train leaves at half past three.

In the next example, the departure date has a low confidence score, so this attribute is confirmed:

    U0: Hello, I want to go from Burgos to Bilbao on March the second

    U0: (DEPART-HOUR) * [0.97, 0.92]

      ORIGIN: Burgos * [0.97, 0.92]

      DESTINATION: Bilbao * [0.87, 0.82]

      DEPART-DATE: 02-03-2004 * [0.36, 0.33]

    S0: Do you want to leave on March the second?

Indeed, by using confidence scores in this way, it is possible to generate detailed replies that contain some values to be confirmed and exclude others, and to use different confirmation strategies such as implicit confirmation for values with relatively high confidence scores and explicit confirmation for those with low scores.

3.3   SUMMARY

The main issues in error handling for spoken dialogue systems include the detection of errors in the user's input and the application of strategies for correcting the errors. Detection of errors has usually been based on acoustic confidence scores associated with the user's input, although a number of other measures have also been used, such as evidence from the user's response to the system's verifications—also known as "late detection of errors." However, using confidence scores requires the appropriate setting of thresholds for acceptance and rejection, which raises the question of whether there is some principled means of setting thresholds that can be learned from data. Similarly, decisions about whether and how to correct errors need to be based on criteria such as the costs and benefits of using a particular strategy. The decisions are likely to vary across different dialogue contexts and consequently would be difficult to handcraft as rules, whereas they could be learned from data and applied using more robust probabilistic methods.

•   •   •   •

CHAPTER 4

Case Studies: Advanced Approaches to Dialogue Management

In this chapter, we take a closer look at some systems and system frameworks that implement and extend the various dialogue control strategies and models introduced in Chapter 2. We begin with Information State Theory, which is an influential method for representing complex information in the Dialogue Context Model. After this, we present an example of the plan-based approach to dialogue in Section 4.2, This approach implements methods for plan recognition and plan generation developed in artificial intelligence (AI), and it is exemplified by work at the University of Rochester in the TRAINS and TRIPS projects. In Section 4.3, we illustrate software agent-based approaches to dialogue management. The focus in these approaches is mainly on the architecture of the dialogue system as a collection of dialogue agents, and they are illustrated through two case studies: the Queen's Communicator (QC) and the AthosMail system. The final (Section 4.4) discusses case studies of dialogue systems developed using mainly statistical methods—the Conversational Architectures Project, which presents a computational model of grounding and a treatment of dialogue as a process of decision making under uncertainty, and the DIHANA system, which illustrates corpus-based dialogue management.

4.1   INFORMATION STATE APPROACH

The Information State approach is a way to model dialogues by specifying them as information states that are updated in the course of the dialogue according to the exchanged contributions as well as certain conditions. The theoretical basis of the information state approach can be found in the update semantics presented by Ginzburg (1996), and in the views of the dialogue being characterized with the help of dialogue acts and speaker obligations that set up options for the speakers at any given point in the dialogue to affect the partner's mental state (beliefs and intentions) in order to build a shared understanding of the tasks and goals of the dialogue. Ginzburg relates dialogue dynamics to the semantics of individual utterances, especially questions, and talks about Questions Under Discussion (QUD) as the main concept in the dialogue modeling. These are the issues that the dialogue participant intends to know about or has brought to the attention of the partner to be resolved during the dialogue.

The information state is akin to the frame in frame-based dialogue control models, but it also contains the values of many parameters that add to the complexity and sophistication of the dialogue model. For instance, it includes the mental states of the speakers that allows more sophisticated reasoning about the dialogue continuation and the preconditions of dialogue acts than is possible by simply reasoning about the filling of a slot in the frame, and the contextual information is richer than the slots in a frame. The task structure can also be represented with a tree instead of a flat list of slots, which supports richer domain information and robust task management.

Different implementations of the Information State approach are available. The TrindiKit (Larsson and Traum, 2000) is a Prolog-based toolkit that is used to implement, for example, the Gothenburg Dialogue System (GODIS). This is an implementation of Ginzburg's original QUD dialogue theory. Another implementation is DIPPER (Bos et al., 2003), which uses a specific update language and also supports declarative representations of dialogue context. The approach is also called Information State Update (ISU) approach with the notion of an Issues Raised (IR) list, that is, a list of IRs in the dialogue so far corresponding to the QUD (Lemon and Gruenstein, 2004). The implementations are based on the Open Agent Architecture (OAA), which provides a flexible architecture where multiple asynchronous communicating processes can be coordinated so as to allow the dynamic, mixed-initiative nature of the dialogues to be managed. We can also mention dialogue games (Carletta et al., 1996) as a version of the information state approach, although this is usually considered a separate theoretical framework as such. However, in dialogue games, the participants make dialogue moves (or conversational moves) based on their goals and given that certain suitable conditions hold at a particular state of the dialogue game, and the dialogue situation is updated according to the move, this is similar to the basic process of ISUs. The Constructive Dialogue Model approach (Jokinen, 2009) is also based on similar premises and the construction of shared context.

In general, dialogue dynamics is implemented by updating the dialogue state information with the help of update rules and dialogue moves. The dialogue moves are understood as triggers for updates, which are then implemented using update rules and an update strategy, and they can be initiated by both the user and the system, that is, mixed-initiative dialogues are allowed. The update rules specify how the information state is updated when a dialogue move is performed, taking into account the move's applicability conditions and effects. A dialogue move might be a dialogue act such as a question, an answer, or a clarification, or it may be a system act such as an information retrieval from the database or a presentation of information to the user. However, an important aspect of the information state approach is that the dialogue moves refer to the grounding of information that is conveyed by the utterance, and thus the notion of dialogue acts is basically used as a convenient label for the inference process rather than a primitive in the dialogue modeling.

Another important part of dialogue management is the QUD stack, or the IR stack, which represents those issues that are not yet resolved or discussed in the dialogue. It is used to drive the dialogue forward. The participants may also have private lists of issues, usually called the speaker's agenda, which they intend to raise in the conversation, and which can be different from each other and from the public list. An issue in the speaker's private agenda can be made public by an utterance (a dialogue move) by the speaker, and it is then moved onto the public QUD/IR stack. Lemon and Gruenstein (2004) notice that the stack is too constrained for move processing in general, and they suggest the use of a dialogue move tree to allow navigation among the subdialogues and topics.

The information state represents the information in a given state of a dialogue, and it includes the mental states of the speakers, that is, their beliefs and intentions, and also other relevant information of the common ground and dialogue context. The context can be rather complex containing information about dialogue acts, grounded concepts, and salient discourse referents. Information states can be defined as recursive feature structures as shown in Figure 4.1. In this figure, the feature structure consists of private and shared parts, representing information that is the agent's private knowledge and information that is assumed to be shared (public) between the dialogue participants, respectively. The agent has its own plan, agenda, and a set of beliefs as well as temporary information about the current dialogue state, and the agent shares with the partner a set of beliefs, the QUD stack, and a list of utterances or previous dialogue moves.

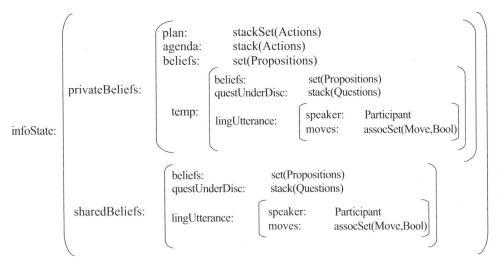

FIGURE 4.1: An information state in the GODIS system (Larsson and Traum, 2000).

When a suitable dialogue move is applied to a dialogue state, the results of the application make up the next, updated information state. The Dialogue Manager has a collection of update rules that interpret the input from the partners with respect to the current information state, and then the state is updated accordingly. The update rules concern dialogue act processing and the system's actions with respect to the application, and they include a part that specifies the requirements that must hold in the information state for the rule to be successfully applied, and a set of statements that describe what the situation will be like after the application of the rule. The rules and conditions can vary in their complexity, and their order of application is handled by the control structure.

In summary, the Information State approach is a powerful approach for modeling complex issues in dialogues, and it includes rich possibilities of flexible dialogue management. By making distinctions between discourse context and the common ground of the speakers, the speakers' beliefs and intentions, and supporting a more flexible presentation of the task structure, the approach allows dialogue management in more complex applications than straightforward information providing applications. These applications typically concern planning and negotiation, or they deal with dynamically changing situations that require sophisticated reasoning and robust dialogue management so as to navigate back and forth among the various dialogue topics and possible alternatives. The Information State approach is in many theoretical (and practical) ways similar to the plan-based approach (to be discussed next), especially in that both aim at sophisticated dialogue agent modeling. The main difference is in the starting point for dialogue management: the Information State approach emphasizes the notion of common ground and the updates for the dialogue state as a means to build shared understanding, whereas the plan-based approaches focus on planning and the speaker's plan recognition as the driving force for dialogues.

4.2   PLAN-BASED APPROACHES

Plan-based approaches to dialogue are based on the notion that agents in a dialogue are attempting to achieve a goal, which may be a physical state, such as arriving at some destination, or a mental state, such as knowing some information. A plan to achieve a goal usually involves a sequence of acts in which the effects of performing an act A can be a precondition for performing some subsequent act B. These acts may be physical acts, but utterances in a dialogue (also known as speech acts, dialogue acts, or communicative acts) can be modeled in a similar manner to physical acts. The following is an example of the communicative act *ConvinceByInform* (Allen, 1995):

Roles:	Speaker, Hearer, Prop
Constraints:	Agent(Speaker), Agent(Hearer), Proposition(Prop), Bel(Speaker,Prop)
Preconditions:	At(Speaker, Loc(Hearer))
Effects:	Bel(Hearer,Prop)

With this communicative act, if a speaker informs a hearer of some proposition and convinces the hearer of that proposition, one constraint (a condition that must be true) is that the speaker must believe the proposition. A precondition of the act—which if not true, can be made true through a further action—is that the speaker should be at the same location as the hearer (for face-to-face communication). As a result of the communicative act, the hearer will believe the proposition. A plan to achieve a goal involving language would typically involve chaining together a series of such communicative acts, including acts that involve representing the intentions and communicative actions of another agent. Allen (1995) provided a detailed account of the planning underlying a simple dialogue concerned with the purchase of a train ticket. Part of this plan involved the agent purchasing the ticket, which involved finding out the price of the ticket from the clerk, which in turn required the clerk to produce a ConvinceByInform act stating the price of the ticket. To achieve this, the agent buying the ticket had to produce a MotivateByRequest act that had as its effect an intention on the part of the clerk to produce the required ConvinceByInform act.

The plan-based approach has been used as a basis for modeling conversational agency in the TRAINS and TRIPS projects at the University of Rochester (Allen et al., 2001a, 2001b). In this work, dialogue is modeled as collaboration between two agents—the human and the system—to achieve a task, which neither of them is able to solve on their own. Based on their current beliefs about the domain, including nested beliefs about shared knowledge, and the discourse obligations that each conversational agent has, each agent selects communicative goals, decides what speech act to perform next, generates an utterance, analyzes the other agent's response, and updates their beliefs about the discourse state and their own discourse obligations. This model of conversational agency is based on the Belief–Desire–Intention (BDI) model of agency, which has been adapted to model conversational actions (Allen, 1995).

The following example illustrates the problem solving and reasoning activities modeled in the TRIPS system (Allen et al., 2001a, p. 30):

U1: We need to get the woman in Penfield to Strong.
S1: OK.
U2: What vehicles are available?
S2: There are ambulances in Pittsford and Webster.
U3: OK. Use one from Pittsford.
S3: Do you know that Route 96 is blocked due to construction?
U4: Oh. Let's use the interstate instead.
S4: OK. I'll dispatch the crew.

This dialogue shows how the system and user engage in dialogue to solve a real-world task that involves moving an injured woman from the town of Penfield to a hospital called Strong. Pittsford and Webster are names of other towns. The dialogue demonstrates the reasoning that is required to participate in such problem solving. The system must be able to reason that the blocking of Route 96 constitutes a possible impediment to the plan proposed by the user. At a more subtle level, the system has to interpret words such as "vehicles" in **U2** according to the appropriate context. In this context, "vehicles" is interpreted as meaning "ambulances," whereas in another context the vehicles could be some other form of transport, such as electric utility trucks.

Figure 4.2 presents the TRIPS architecture (based on Allen et al., 2001b, p. 3). Although it looks complicated at first, it maps to the basic dialogue system architecture presented in Figure 1.1, in that, for instance, the main components to handle spoken language understanding and response generation are handled by the Interpretation and Generation Managers. However, in addition to these, the TRIPS architecture divides Dialogue Manager into a Behavioral Agent (BA), which plans the system's behavior, a Generation Manager (GM), which takes care of the system's response generation, and a Task Manager, which manages task- and domain-specific knowledge sources, and a specific Discourse Context, which takes care of the dialogue history, discourse referents, and user and the system beliefs. (cf. also the Interact/AthosMail architecture in Section 4.3.2).

Interpretation in the TRIPS system goes beyond the methods discussed so far since it requires intention recognition to interpret the outputs of the Automatic Speech Recognition (ASR) and Spoken Language Understanding (SLU) components in terms of the dialogue context. SLU in TRIPS involves a feature-based augmented context-free grammar with an agenda-driven, best-first chart parser. The SLU component returns a set of speech acts, for example,

ok (ack) let's do that then (accept) send a truck to Avon (request)

These are then interpreted in terms of how they relate to the current plan and the system's discourse obligations (Traum and Allen 1994) that have arisen as a consequence of the speech acts that are identified. For example, an utterance such as "do you know that Route 96 is blocked due to construction" might be interpreted in one context as a problem statement with the intention of initiating a change of plan (as in the dialogue quoted earlier involving moving an injured woman from Penfield). In another context, the utterance might simply be interpreted as an attempt to update the user's knowledge. The Task Manager may be used to help with the interpretation of intended speech acts and problem solving acts, by relating what the user is saying or doing to the task at hand.

The IM works in close collaboration with the Discourse Context, which provides information about the state of the dialogue, including the entities that have been mentioned, a representation of the structure and interpretation of the immediately preceding utterance, a discourse history of the speech acts so far and whether they have been grounded (or confirmed), and the system's

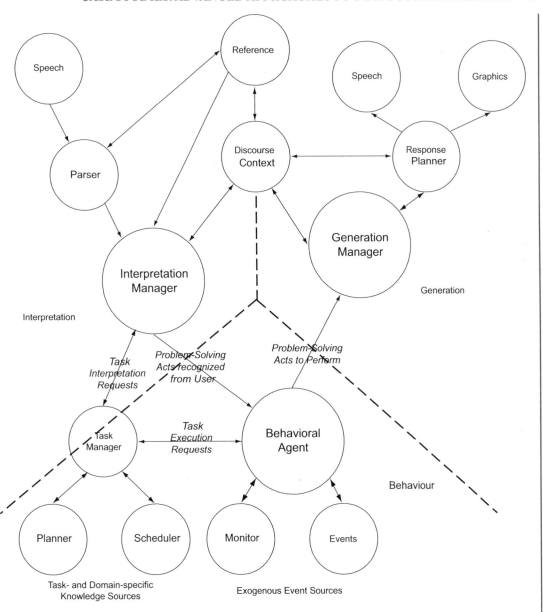

FIGURE 4.2: The TRIPS architecture.

current obligations—for example, whether the system has an obligation to respond to the user's last utterance. After each utterance, the Discourse Context is updated.

The TRIPS system makes use of various methods to ensure robust performance of the interpretation process. Speech recognition errors are corrected using a statistical model of the recognizer's past performance in the domain, including typical substitutions that had occurred as errors in the past and a word bigram model based on transcribed dialogues with the system that is used to predict likely sequences of words. In cases where the parser is unable to interpret the complete input from the user, robust parsing strategies are applied that can match at different levels of specificity with partial or ill-formed input. For example,

> Spoken sentence:
> *Okay let's take the train from Detroit to Washington*
> Recognized sentence:
> *Okay let's send contain from Detroit to Washington*
> Speech act sequence:
> *1. CONFIRM / ACKNOWLEDGE ("Okay")*
> *2. TELL (involving some interpretable words: "let's send contain")*
> *3. TELL (mentions a route: "from Detroit to Washington").*

In this example, the parser has extracted enough information to allow the IM to perform some interpretation, for example, identification of objects mentioned, before passing on the acts to the BA to perform verbal reasoning. In this example, the third speech act could be a suggestion to move from Detroit to Washington. To check if this is plausible, the BA needs to check that there is an engine at Detroit. As this is the case, the interpretation is accepted and the Discourse Context is updated.

As far as dialogue control is concerned, the dialogue evolves dynamically as a result of interactions between BA and other components of the system. The BA is responsible for problem solving within the system, including interpreting user utterances and actions in terms of problem solving acts, keeping track of the system's goals and obligations during the course of problem solving, and dealing with changes in the world state—for example, incoming news of Route 96 being blocked, which may affect a plan previously developed or currently under discussion. The BA uses a general abstract model that is applicable to all dialogues involving practical problem solving. This model includes concepts such as "objectives" (goals, subgoals, constraints), "solutions" (plans), "resources" (available objects for the solutions), and "situations" (how the world is currently).

The BA works in conjunction with the Task Manager. Whereas the behaviors of the BA are defined in terms of a general and abstract problem solving model, the Task Manager is concerned with objects and actions in a specific domain. For example, in the emergency rescue scenario illustrated in the example above, an ambulance is considered a "resource" and moving the injured woman to a hospital is part of a "solution" within the scenario.

The BA also has to consider its goals and obligations. The dialogue agent will have a set of goals to pursue, such as obtaining information from the user. At the same time, the agent will have a number of obligations, such as responding to the user's utterances. A simple example would be when an agent is attempting to elicit the various items of information for a flight booking and the user interrupts with a query about hotels. The agent has to decide whether to continue with its own agenda or whether to allow the user to shift the topic. Even when the agent decides to pursue its own agenda, it must at least fulfill the conversational obligation of acknowledging the user's attempt to shift topic (e.g., by saying something like "I'll come back to hotels in a minute").

TRIPS uses a reactive–deliberative model of dialogue agency (Traum, 1996). Where there is a conflict between the agent's goals and obligations, the agent displays a "relaxed" conversational style in which discourse obligations are addressed before the agent's own goals. This gives rise to an interaction in which the initiative of the other agent is followed. However, in a less cooperative situation, the agent can continue to address its discourse obligations but can respond in different ways, for example, by rejecting requests and refusing to answer questions. Thus, depending on the flow of the dialogue and on the behavior of the other agent, the dialogue agent can shift its focus from the obligation-driven process of following the other's initiative to the goal-driven process of taking the lead in the conversation. There may also be occasions when the dialogue agent's strategy is determined by exogenous events, such as incoming news that might affect how the current task can be solved. The agent must decide whether to interrupt the ongoing dialogue to inform the user of this event and whether to adopt an intention to propose a solution or leave the solution to the user. In **S3** above, the agent informed the user of some important new information but left it to the user to formulate a new plan.

The GM is also more complex than in the systems presented earlier. In deciding what to say, GM takes two sources of information into account:

- The problem solving goals provided by the BA that require generation
- The discourse obligations from the Discourse Context

The GM constructs discourse acts for generation and sends these with their associated context to the Response Planner, which produces a surface representation for generation. If there is no available information from the IM or the BA to communicate at a particular point in the dialogue, the GM can use basic dialogue rules to acknowledge the user's utterance and perform some basic grounding. When the GM has successfully produced a discourse act, the Discourse Context is updated.

In summary, TRIPS implements a model of conversational agency in which the dialogue evolves dynamically as the system and user collaborate to construct a plan. The plan is developed incrementally in order to incorporate new constraints that arise during the course of the dialogue, either because of external events or as a result of suggestions for alternative solutions by either participant. Although this type of dialogue behavior could, in principle, be modeled using scripted dialogue management model, the problem is that it would be burdensome. The power of plan-based dialogue management is that the dialogue logic can be specified more compactly using plans, which implement the script-type control of possible dialogue states but can be instantiated in various ways without explicitly enumerating all the possibilities in advance as is the case in predetermined scripts.

4.3   SOFTWARE AGENTS FOR DIALOGUE MANAGEMENT

The term "agent" is rather ambiguous in dialogue management research. It can refer to intelligent dialogue agents, which model intelligent autonomous behavior with cognitive attitudes such as beliefs, desires, and intentions, and incorporate AI techniques such as planning, cooperation, and inferencing to simulate interaction between intelligent agents. These autonomous agents are usually called BDI (Belief-Desire-Intention) agents, so as to refer to the intelligent behavior models. Many earlier dialogue systems aimed at BDI-type dialogue modeling and the dialogue management was designed to deploy rules and contextual knowledge to interpret and generate appropriate system behaviors. For instance, the Artimis system (Sadek et al., 1997), the PLUS system (Black et al., 1991), and many Expert systems (Moore and Swartout, 1989) were of this type. Also, the TRIPS system, presented in Section 4.2, is an example of this type of intelligent dialogue agent.

On the other hand, there is also another use of the term "agent-based" dialogue system. This refers to software agents where the "agents" are conceived as software objects that perform particular functions in the interaction. Most current research systems are software agent-based systems, since the object-oriented programming has become a standard means of implementing interactive systems. Examples of such software agent-based dialogue systems are Galaxy Communicator (Seneff et al., 1998; Rudnicky et al., 1999) and OAA (Martin et al., 1998).

In this section, we discuss this type of software agent-based dialogue management and the issues concerning software agent communication, control, and architecture. We present two dialogue systems, the Queen's Communicator (QC) and the AthosMail system, as case studies of the software agent-based dialogue management. Both of them implement a frame-based dialogue control with an elaborated structure of nested software agents, asynchronous processing, and control of information flow, and communication between the software agents.

4.3.1   The Queen's Communicator

The QC handles transactions in the domains of accommodation requests and bookings as well as event requests and bookings (theater and cinema). The Dialogue Manager supports mixed-initiative dialogue, in which the user can supply more information than requested by the system and in which the user can correct the system or change information that has already been elicited, if they so desire. A mixture of explicit and implicit confirmation strategies are used, depending on the current state of the dialogue, and the system may perform a combination of confirming and validating the elicited information as well as requesting additional information in a single turn. The system also supports domain switching, so that, for example, the user can switch to a request about cinema information while negotiating an accommodation dialogue.

The overall system architecture is based on the MIT/Mitre Galaxy Communicator architecture, which was designed to support a plug-and-play approach to dialogue systems development (Seneff et al., 1998). In this architecture, a number of servers (components) interact with each other through the Defense Advanced Research Projects Agency hub, passing messages, in the form of frames, to the hub. The hub acts as a router, sending frames to the receiving server. The actions of the hub are controlled by a simple script. Different servers can be plugged into the architecture. More specifically, QC builds on the CU (University of Colorado) version of the architecture (Pellom et al., 2001) but with an object-based Dialogue Manager that is implemented as a suite of Java classes (O'Neill et al., 2005).

Dialogue management is conceived as an Expertise Hierarchy comprising components that the system uses to implement its generic confirmation strategies (i.e., what to do when the user supplies new, modified, or negated information), and its domain-specific, dialogue-furthering strategies (e.g., what to ask for next in an accommodation inquiry, or a theater reservation, or when eliciting credit card details). The DialogManager has a suite of EnquiryExperts, such as an Accommodation Expert and an EventExpert, as well as a DomainSpotter that helps select domain expertise, and a DiscourseHistory that maintains a record of user–system interaction across domains. The Enquiry-Experts are organized in terms of a hierarchy of expertise in which more specialized agents inherit a common core of discourse management behaviors, ensuring that all agents use a common discourse style. Each agent encapsulates a specific role, such as collecting a telephone number or performing some action, and in combination with other agents accomplishes domain-specific transactions and inquiries. Within each category, the agents can be further refined into more specific hierarchies. For example, a payment agent could be refined into another agent that deals with very specific forms of payment, such as a store credit card. This hierarchical representation supports a dynamically evolving dialogue that can progress from a general to a more specific interaction. Likewise, in the case of an unsuccessful inquiry, it is possible to back off from interaction with a specific to a more general agent.

The Domain Spotter has an overall controlling function and is responsible for handling user interaction, assigning the user's requests to the most appropriate agent, and handling requests between agents. All interagent discourse requests are handled in terms of a statement of desired expertise rather than in terms of a specific requested agent. Agents are registered with the Domain Spotter, so that their expertise is made available to the wider system. Given an incoming user request, for example, for a hotel booking, the Domain Spotter selects agents to poll for the agent that best fulfills the request.

The system's Dialogue Context Model takes the form of a collection of DialogFrame objects, which are similar to the frames used in frame-based systems, in that they represent the slots that need to be filled in order to complete a transaction. However, in the QC these slots contain the following additional information:

- The "confirmation status" of attributes—This is a measure of the status of the attributes within the dialogue (Heisterkamp and McGlashan, 1996). For example, information can be "NEW_FOR_SYSTEM", "INFERRED_BY_SYSTEM", "REPEATED_BY_USER", "MODIFIED_BY_USER", "NEGATED_BY_USER", "MODIFIED_BY_SYSTEM", or "NEGATED_BY_SYSTEM".
- The discourse peg of attributes—This is a score used to ensure that every attribute has been adequately confirmed before it is used to further a transaction.

For example, the following is an attribute within a DialogFrame

Attribute (Hilton, NEW_FOR_SYSTEM, 0, confirm)

This attribute indicates that the slot value "Hilton" has the confirmation status of NEW_FOR_SYSTEM with a discourse peg of 0, and a system intention to confirm the value.

Completion of a transaction requires that key information is reconfirmed. To ensure that this is the case, the discourse pegs for key pieces of information have to be set greater than 1. Every attribute uttered by the user must be repeated once or explicitly confirmed by the user to be considered confirmed by the system. Attributes that are negated or changed by the user are queried before they are considered adequately confirmed. Only confirmed attribute values are considered for use with the system's request templates and associated rules. To achieve this, discourse pegs are incremented by 1 when the user repeats a value, zeroed if the value is modified, and set to −1 if the value is negated.

The confirmation status and discourse peg are used to determine the system's intentions. The principal intentions are "CONFIRM" (for new values), "REPAIR_CONFIRM" (for a modified value), "REPAIR_REQUEST" (for a negated value), and "SPECIFY" (to have the user specify a required value). Once a particular level of confirmation has been reached (a "confirmedness threshold"), the system can decide how to use information supplied by the user—for example, to complete or to further the transaction.

Frames can be linked together to form larger discourse objects that model a complete transaction. For example, a theater inquiry may require linkage to a credit card frame representing payment information. These links are not predetermined but evolve dynamically over the course of the dialogue.

Interpretation in QC is based on the output from the ASR and the SLU components that is used to identify the domain relevant to the query and to populate the appropriate DialogFrame. Dialogue control is a dynamic process that is determined by the information in the DialogFrame. The following annotated example (extracted from O'Neill et al., 2005, pp. 119–120) illustrates these processes.

U1: I'd like to book a four-star hotel in Belfast from the fifteenth of December to the twentieth of December.

    Recognized Input = FOUR-STAR HOTEL BELFAST FROM 15TH DECEMBER
    TO 20TH DECEMBER

Key words like four-star and hotel help identify the accommodation domain. The DomainSpotter appoints the AccommodationExpert as the "handling agent." The AccommodationExpert populates its AccommodationDialogFrame with whatever relevant information has been supplied by the user.

S2a: Ok, let's start a new accommodation booking—that's a four-star hotel in Belfast from 15th December until 20th December. Please wait while I check the database . . .

The AccommodationExpert confirms the new values that it has identified, and uses its own domain-specific rules to initiate a database lookup that will retrieve names of hotels that match the user's criteria.

S2b: You can choose between the following: the Europa, the Malone Lodge, the Stormont, or the Holiday Inn. Which would you prefer?

U2: Could you make that a three-star?

    Recognized Input = THREE-STAR

Although the system in its utterance has strongly suggested that the user should select one of the hotel names it has retrieved from the database, this is a mixed-initiative system, so the user may provide information different to that which was requested. In this case, the user changes the star-rating required. As a result of the user changing the original value, the confirmation status of the attribute AccoClass changes to MODIFIED_BY_USER with a new system intention for this attribute of REPAIR_CONFIRM. Changes are also made to other attributes, such as AccoType, Location, DateFrom, and DateTo: the pegs have been incremented and the status changed to REPEATED_BY_USER. This status is assigned on the basis that these values are now considered to have been implicitly confirmed by the user since they were not modified when the user modified the value AccoClass.

S3: OK, got it. So that's a three-star. Is that correct?

Using its inherited confirmation strategy, the AccommodationExpert compares the value for the star-rating in the previous frame with the star-rating in the current frame and performs a "repair-confirm" on the changed value.

In summary, the object-based dialogue management implemented in the QC provides certain advantages over other approaches. From a dialogue engineering perspective, the object-oriented design methodology provides benefits in terms of improved maintainability, extensibility, and reusability, as well as in terms of limiting the degree of structural decay as the system evolves and changes over time (Hanna et al., 2007). In terms of dialogue management, the approach enables experts (or agents) to be identified that can appropriately handle the user's utterances along with strategies for furthering the dialogue and dealing with confirmations and repairs. Although QC uses a slot-filling approach to manage the information conveyed in the dialogue, the additional information contained in the DialogFrames concerning the confirmation status and the discourse peg of the attributes along with the rules encapsulated in the EnquiryExpert objects provides for a dynamically evolving, mixed-initiative dialogue that crosses several transaction domains.

4.3.2   AthosMail System

The AthosMail system is a multilingual spoken dialogue system for reading e-mail messages, developed in the DUMAS (Dynamic Universal Mobility for Adaptive Speech Interfaces) project (Jokinen and Gambäck, 2004). It includes components for input interpretation, dialogue management, semantic template construction, user modeling, and random indexing, and its key features are adaptivity and the integration of different approaches for spoken interaction.

The AthosMail application (Turunen et al., 2004) is based on the Jaspis architecture (Turunen et al., 2006), which has been applied in a range of application areas, including the bus timetable system Interact (Jokinen et al., 2002), the multimodal route navigation system MUMS (Hurtig and Jokinen, 2006), and a mobile route guidance system (Turunen et al., 2006). The Jaspis architecture is similar to the Galaxy II architecture in that it consists of a number of components that are connected to a central manager. However, each component consists of a manager and a set of agents and evaluators that implement the dialogue functionalities. The notion of an agent may be confusing since the Jaspis agents are not agents in the sense of typical agent architectures, that is, the type that encapsulate expertise for a particular task as, for example, in the QC, nor are they autonomous BDI agents as in plan-based AI systems. Rather, the Jaspis agents describe actions available for the manager to handle different dialogue situations that might arise, such as the generation of explicit or implicit confirmation, selection of system- or user-initiative dialogue, navigating among folders and messages, and providing context-sensitive help. In AthosMail, there are more than 50 "agents."

The evaluators, on the other hand, determine the action for each dialogue and select the agent that can best handle a particular dialogue situation. Thus they correspond to typical intelligent software agents.

An example of the operation of agents and evaluators is depicted in Figure 4.3. The agents, in this case representing different dialogue acts, are scored on the basis of their applicability within a given dialogue situation, and the CanHandleEvaluator selects the agent that receives the highest score to deal with the current dialogue situation. In the heuristic agent selection, the agents assign scores to themselves on the basis of investigating the dialogue state and how well they are applicable to it, and the selection of the best agent is made dynamically based on scores that are compared by the evaluator. Kerminen and Jokinen (2003) also showed that agent selection could be interpreted as action selection of autonomous agents, and implemented using a reinforcement learning algorithm. The right-hand side of Figure 4.3 shows agent selection based on reinforcement learning. Now, the evaluator is replaced by a Q-estimate evaluator, which chooses the agent that has proven to be the most rewarding so far, according to a Q-learning algorithm (Sutton and Barto, 1998), cf. Section 2.2.4.

The high-level AthosMail architecture with the main modules of the online Dialogue System is depicted in Figure 4.4. Information about the system state, such as the dialogue history and user profiles, is kept in a shared knowledge base (Information Storage), which can be accessed by each module through the Information Manager. Interaction among the modules is coordinated by the Interaction Manager. The e-mail interfacing system consists of an online and an offline part, that communicate over an XML–RPC interface. The offline system is necessary because some of the techniques used for message processing (in particular, classification and clustering) require offline resources.

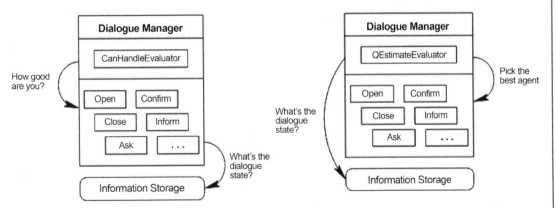

FIGURE 4.3: Heuristic agent selection (left) and reinforcement-based learning (right) in the Interact system (Kerminen and Jokinen, 2003).

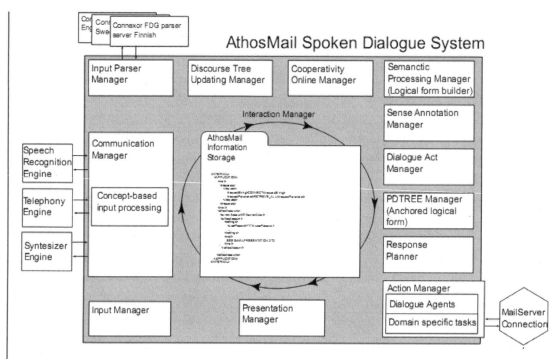

FIGURE 4.4: The AthosMail architecture. From Turunen et al. (2004).

The interpretation of the user's input is coordinated by the Input Manager and Input Parser Manager. Their tasks include the selection and creation of the input vocabulary in terms of recognition grammars or language models, and the selection of the required natural language grammars to handle the user's spoken input (in AthosMail, different speech recognizers and parsers are used to handle English, Swedish, and Finnish input). The Semantic Processing, Sense Annotation, and Discourse Tree Updating Managers take care of the discourse handling and semantic processing of the input, and the system also includes managers that are concerned with the selection of the dialogue actions (DialogueAct Manager) and the system actions (Action Manager). A distinguishing feature of AthosMail is the Cooperativity Manager, which implements a user model and adaptation of the system according to the user's competence level. The Cooperativity Model records the user's actions and estimates the user's expertise concerning the use of the application on the basis of the dialogue history, the user's previous behavior, and the current context. The system tailors its responses according to the user's expertise level, so that the novice user will receive longer responses that provide more information about the alternative actions that the user can take at the current dialogue state, whereas the expert user will only be presented with the new information and not be bored with information that they already know. The model consists of an online and an offline component, the former calculating runtime expertise recommendations, and the latter calculating default expertise values based on long-time observations of the user's behavior. A more detailed description is given by Jokinen and Kanto (2004) and Jokinen (2006).

An example of an AthosMail dialogue is given below. The user is an expert user and the system responses do not contain any unnecessary help information.

S: Welcome to the AthosMail system. Please enter your four digit user code.

U: XXXX [DTMF]

S: Please give your secret passcode.

U: XXXX [DTMF]

S: Please wait, connecting to your mail server.

S: Hi, Test user. No new messages. 17 old messages. Listing groups. You have five groups.

   Group one, messages with subject "Reply: about deliverables."

   Group two, messages from Adam Funk.

   Three, messages from Kristiina Jokinen.

   Four, messages from Kari Kanto.

   Fifth contains miscellaneous messages.

U: Select the third group

S: Group three contains three messages from Kristiina Jokinen.

   Subject of the first message is: "D6.1."

   Subject of the second message is: "telemeeting on Tuesday 21/10."

   Subject of the third message is: "Deliverables due!!"

U: I'd like to hear more information about the third message

S: Message number one from Kristiina Jokinen, subject is "Deliverables due." Message was sent on Wednesday at 14.24. It has six lines. Summary of message: "Deliverables due this Friday"

U: What messages do I have from Adam Funk?

S: Group two contains four messages from Adam Funk.

   Subject of the first message is: "AthosMail review, urgent."

   Subject of the second message is: "Reply: Running AthosMail."

   Subject of the third message is: "Reply: SICStus Bug report (SPRM 5425)."

   Subject of the fourth message is: "AthosMail: Integrating the generator."

   You can choose a message saying for example first message or second message.

U: Read the first message

S: Message with the subject "AthosMail review, urgent," sent by Adam Funk.

   Quote from the previous message: Do you have everything ready? Quote ends.

   Our components are finished. I made a draft of changes. You can find it at the webpage. Cheers, Adam.

The message has been read.

U: Delete it

S: Please confirm that message "AthosMail review, urgent," send by Adam Funk, is to be deleted. Answer yes or no.

U: Yes

S: The message has been marked for deletion. It will be deleted when you logout.

No new messages. 17 old messages, one message marked for deletion.

U: Thank you and bye!

S: Do you want to quit now? Please say yes or no.

U: Yes

S: Bye, please call again.

The AthosMail architecture has no central component that makes decisions about dialogue management, but dialogue control is distributed over different components as in the TRIPS architecture (cf. Section 4.2). The implemented dialogue systems manifest an approach called distributed dialogue management (Kerminen and Jokinen 2003). In this manner, the dialogue functionalities are distributed across specialized components with no predefined execution order, enabling greater flexibility and adaptivity.

In summary, the AthosMail architecture facilitates adaptive and flexible dialogue control through the use of the agents–managers–evaluators paradigm, and supports distributed dialogue management whereby dialogue control is distributed among the system components. There can also be different "agents" or action alternatives for the same task, for example, to provide speech output in different languages, or to choose different action paths through the system. New functionalities can be added by adding new managers with appropriate agents and evaluators, and different behaviors can be modeled by specifying alternative agents for the same task. This is especially useful in an adaptive system like AthosMail, where the user model is dynamically updated during the dialogue.

In general, the software agent-based approaches facilitate adaptive and flexible dialogue control through the use of multiple software agents as is exemplified via the two systems, QC and AthosMail. Application development times can be shortened as the use of existing configurable component libraries allows the developers to concentrate on the novel challenging aspects of dialogue management. However, it is often necessary to redefine the existing components and to modify conditions for the agent selection due to a modified component set. Thus, the agent-based approach also poses interesting questions about task decomposition: what are the smallest parameterized actions that are needed for composing various tasks, and which can be used as reusable agents in dialogue systems?

4.4   THE CONVERSATIONAL ARCHITECTURES PROJECT

The Conversational Architectures Project implemented a computational model of grounding in which conversation was modeled as a process of decision making under uncertainty (Paek and Horvitz, 1999, 2000). The system reasoned about sources of error and applied a costs/benefits analysis to determine whether to resolve the error and which actions to take.

The model of communication, which has been adopted in a number of other studies (e.g., Bohus, 2007; Skantze, 2007), involves four levels of representation:

- *Channel.* This level is concerned with the channel of communication between S and L. To communicate, S will attempt to open a channel of communication with L by displaying some behavior, such as an utterance or a gesture. For communication to be successful at this level, L must attend to S.
- *Signal.* This level is concerned with the signal that is presented from S to L. S and L have to agree that a behavior was intended as a signal, as some behaviors, such as adjusting spectacles, are not normally intended as signals.
- *Intention.* The intention level involves the semantic content of signals. At this level, S signals some message to L, and L has to determine the intentions behind this message.
- *Conversation.* At the conversation level, S proposes a joint activity for L to consider and take up.

Each level requires coordination between a speaker S and a listener L, so that each participant is assured that the other(s) are attending, hearing, understanding, and cooperating with what is being said. Grounding is required at each level. Moreover, actions at all four levels of representation involve uncertainty. At the lowest level, S may not be sure whether L is attending, whereas at the signal level the signal may not have been clearly identified. There are costs associated with actions that are carried out to resolve uncertainty at each level. For example, at the channel level the cost of asking for a repeat because L has not been attending is likely to be low compared with the cost of continuing the dialogue without ensuring mutual understanding.

The grounding strategies depend on the type of user utterance that the system is responding to. The following are some of the strategies that are available:

1. No repair
    1.1   Do an action that is relevant to the preceding turn.
    1.2   Assume speech is overheard and so ignore.
    1.3   Wait for further information before deciding.
    1.4   Give positive feedback (acknowledgment).

2. Display confusion (and attempt to elicit repair by user)
   2.1   In a general way.
   2.2   By specifying the grounding level.
3. Confirm understanding
   3.1   Seek clarification.
       3.1.1   In a general way.
       3.1.2   By specifying the grounding level.
   3.2   Declare intention before action.
4. Consider combinations of repair actions
5. Other repairs

For example, a general repair might be something like "so you want a shuttle?" whereas a repair specifying the grounding level (in this case, signal) might be "I'm not sure I heard you correctly—did you want a shuttle?"

Each of the grounding strategies is associated with an expected utility. For example, requesting repetition of an utterance has a high expected utility if on the signal level NO CHANNEL is suspected, as L will not have attended to the utterance. However, repetition has low expected utility if CHANNEL AND SIGNAL OPEN, as the utterance will have been heard and the problem is more likely to be located at a higher level, such as Inference or Conversation Control. Decisions as to which strategy to select are encoded in Decision-Based Transition Networks (DTN), in which transitions are set by decision-theoretic functions. DTNs represent conversational structures such as "adjacency pairs" and the transitions model the probabilities associated with different choices of next response.

4.4.1   Example: Taking Decisions

The following example illustrates how decisions about grounding are taken at the Intention Level. Goals cannot be observed directly, so the system infers a probability distribution over all possible goals given the different types of evidence—linguistic, contextual, and nonlinguistic—that it has available. If the probability of a particular goal given the evidence E, $p_{(Goal|E)}$, does not exceed a given threshold, the system has to decide between two different strategies: Inquire_Goal and Ask_Repair (these strategies are encoded in a DTN). Inquire_Goal asks the user to state their goal explicitly, whereas Ask_Repair uses an embedded sequence (clarification request) to obtain more information.

Considering the strategy of Ask_Repair, probability thresholds are used to decide which version of this strategy to use. Problems at lower levels, such as signal and channel problems, can also affect grounding at the Intention level, and so a probability distribution is obtained over the states represented at the Maintenance Level that are concerned with problems due to channel and signal. Taking this information into account results in selection of the following strategies:

- Ask_Repair (elaboration)—This is used if the probability of channel and signal exceeds a threshold. In other words, it is assumed that the misunderstanding is at the intention level, but a maintenance level problem such as an incorrect parse is not excluded.
- Ask_Repair(repeat)—This is used if the most likely maintenance level state is CHANNEL and NO SIGNAL, as the system may not have received a sufficiently clear signal from the user.
- Ask_Repair(specify)—This strategy uses value-of-information analysis to identify the best signals to observe given the inferred probabilities of different goals. For example, if it is recommended that the word "shuttle" should be observed, the system can make the repair more specific by asking if the request has anything to do with getting a shuttle.

Thus, in order to resolve misunderstandings the system reasons about uncertainties at several different levels of analysis, taking into account the costs and benefits of handling the error in terms of the expected utility of each action.

4.5   CORPUS-BASED DIALOGUE MANAGEMENT: THE DIHANA PROJECT

The corpus-based approach to dialogue management can be illustrated with reference to the DIHANA project, which was concerned with telephone access to Spanish train timetable information and prices (Griol et al., 2006; Hurtado et al., 2006). The corpus was acquired using the Wizard of Oz technique, in which the Wizard played the role of the Dialogue Manager, but the other components of the system, such as the speech recognition and speech understanding modules, were used as such. The Wizard's strategy was concerned with confirmation of user input with low confidence scores using the following rules:

- Safe state
  If the input has a confidence score that is higher than the fixed threshold, the Wizard selects one of the following three interactions:

  1. Implicit confirmation, query to the database, and answer to the user, if the Dialogue Register (DR) (the system's information state) contains all the necessary information.
  2. Inquiry to the user if the DR does not store a value for the current concept and/or some of the minimum attributes.

3. Mixed confirmation to give naturalness to the dialogue, which includes the data to be confirmed and the data with a confidence score that is higher than the fixed threshold.

- Uncertain state
  When one or more data of the DR have a confidence score that is lower than the fixed threshold, the Wizard selects one of the following two interactions:

  1. Explicit confirmation of the first uncertain item that appears in the DR.
  2. Mixed confirmation to give naturalness to the dialogue.

A total of 900 dialogues was collected. The corpus included information about the outputs of the speech recognition and speech understanding modules (with confidence scores), the answer produced by the system, the values of the attributes elicited during the dialogue, and the queries made to the database. The user turns were labeled as dialogue acts using the traditional frame representation to encode the intention of the utterance and the values of the attributes supplied by the user, for example:

Input sentence:
Yes, I would like to know the timetables and the train types leaving from Barcelona.

Semantic interpretation:
(Affirmation)
(Hour)
Origin: Barcelona
(Train-Type)
Origin: Barcelona

The system turns were labeled in terms of dialogue acts that represent the meanings and functions of the utterances, using three levels of acts:

1. General level: Opening, Closing, Undefined, Not-Understood, Waiting, New-Query, Acceptance, Rejection, Question, Confirmation, and Answer
2. Task-dependent concepts and attributes: Departure-Hour, Arrival-Hour, Price, Train-Type, Origin, Destination, Date, Order-Number, Number-Trains, Services, Class, Trip-Type, Trip Time, and Nil
3. The values of the attributes elicited from the user's utterances

Table 4.1 shows some examples of the dialogue act labeling of the system turns.

TABLE 4.1: Dialogue act labeling of system turns (from Hurtado et al., 2006: 50).

USER UTTERANCE	DIALOGUE ACT LABELING
Do you want to know timetables?	(Confirmation:Departure-Hour:Nil)
Do you want train types to Valencia, from Barcelona?	(Confirmation:Train-Type:Destination) (Confirmation:Origin:Origin)
There is only one train, which is a Euromed, that leaves at 0:27 at night. Anything else?	(Answer:Departure-Hour:Departure-Hour, Number-Trains, Train-Type) (New-Query:Nil:Nil)

This labeled corpus was used to estimate the stochastic Dialogue Manager using the sequences of system and user dialogue acts obtained from the training data.

4.5.1   Selecting the Next System Act

The objective of the dialog manager is to find the best system act A_i at each time i, taking into account the preceding states of the dialogue, where each state (S) of a dialogue consists of a pair of system (A) and user (U) turns:

$$\hat{A}_i = \arg\max_{A_i \in A} P(A_i \mid S_1, ..., S_{i-1})$$

However, as with Markov decision processes, taking into account all the preceding states of the dialogue is likely to lead to combinatorial explosion. For this reason, the state space was partitioned through the use of a DR that contained information about the concepts and attributes provided by the user over the previous states of the dialogue. The information in the DR was coded taking only into account whether the user had provided a value for the concept or attribute along with its confidence score. In this way, the complete dialogue history can still be considered.

Different sequences of state spaces that lead to the same DR were considered equivalent. In this way, the state space was reduced at a possible cost of a loss of the chronological sequence of events, although this was not considered significant in this system, which was required to elicit values for a number of data items but not in any particular order. Given the DR, the problem of finding the best system act was specified as:

$$\hat{A}_i = \arg\max_{A_i \in A} P(A_i \mid DR_{i-1}, ..., S_{i-1})$$

Selecting the next system to act in this way works well for sequences of states seen in the training corpus but is problematic when a pair (DR, S) is encountered that was unseen. The following is an example (based on Hurtado et al., 2006):

S1: Welcome to the railway information system. How can I help you?
U1: I want to go to Barcelona.
S2: Do you want to know the timetables?
U2: Yes, for the Euromed train.
S3: Tell me the departure date.
U3: Tomorrow.

At **U2**, an unseen sequence has occurred as there is no (DR, S) in the corpus addressing the attribute Train-Type (Euromed), so the system selects the nearest (DR', S'), which asks about Departure-Date and ignores the fact that the user asked about the type of train (Euromed). Different solutions have been evaluated for selecting the closest pair. In Hurtado et al. (2006), a distance measure was used. In an evaluation of this approach, although more than 25% of the dialogues contained unseen situations, the overall dialogue success rate was 85%. In another solution, the coverage problem was treated as a classification issue, in which all pairs (DR, S) that provide the training corpus in the same system response are assigned to a class. During a new dialogue, each unseen pair is then classified into one of the available classes (i.e., possible system answers). Hurtado et al. (2006) extends the use of this classification to manage both seen and unseen situations, using a multilayer perceptron for the classification process.

4.6   SUMMARY

This chapter has provided several case studies of various dialogue management methods. We first considered the dialogue state approach, and presented the ISU approach, which provides a more extensive version of frame-based dialogue management. Next, we illustrated plan-based approaches that draw on theories of planning from AI, using the TRIPS system as an example. Two examples of the software agent-based systems were also introduced. The QC illustrated how an object-oriented Dialogue Manager could support cross-domain interactions, mixed-initiative dialogue, and a context-sensitive method for selecting methods for confirmation. In AthosMail, the use of multiple agents that are selected dynamically supports a more adaptive and flexible dialogue control. The final sections of the chapter presented systems that make use of decision making under uncertainty and corpus-based approaches to dialogue management.

CHAPTER 5

Advanced Issues

Dialogue technology has developed to a level where practical interactive systems can be built and deployed commercially. However, in order to increase the naturalness and flexibility of the interaction, researchers in spoken dialogue technology are addressing the challenges posed by systems that display more intelligent conversational capabilities. These systems are concerned with modelling the properties and processes of dialogue that go beyond straightforward information exchange. In this chapter, we introduce examples of these more intelligent conversational capabilities, and discuss how these aspects have been implemented in a variety of spoken dialogue systems. We especially focus on cooperation (Section 5.1), adaptation (Section 5.2), and multimodality (Section 5.3), and also briefly discuss natural communication in relation to non-verbal communication studies (Section 5.4).

5.1 COOPERATION AND COMMUNICATIVE COMPETENCE

Cooperation is commonly understood as one of the basic requirements of successful communication. However, it is difficult to explain and formalise the characteristics of cooperative behavior and how cooperation works in actual situations. One of the most cited works in this respect is Grice's Cooperation Principle (Grice, 1975). This is intended to serve the purpose of "maximally effective exchange of information", and it concerns the speaker's presentation of information so that the speaker fulfills the four maxims: Quality (be truthful), Quantity (be informative), Manner (be brief and orderly), and Relation (be relevant). However, the maxims have also been criticized for being too oriented toward dialogues that concern factual information exchanges, and also for being internally contradictory (e.g., the so-called "white lies" go against the maxim of Quality although in the situation they may also follow some aspects of polite manners, whereas the maxims of Quantity and Relation can support opposite aspects as when the former would recommend providing enough but not too much information and the latter would recommend providing all relevant information).

Dialogue cooperation can occur on different levels. In computational research, cooperation and collaboration have been demonstrated in terms of the dialogue partners working together on a particular task (Cohen and Levesque, 1990a, 1990b; Grosz and Sidner, 1990; Rich et al., 2005), on grounding and exchanging information (Clark and Wilkes-Gibbs, 1986; Traum, 1996, 1999; Jokinen, 1996), co-producing utterances (Fais, 1994), and adapting to the partner's lexical items and speaking style (Pickering and Garrod, 2004).

On the most general level, cooperation refers to the partners' ability to work in a helpful and coordinated manner. Collaboration models are usually based on artificial intelligence (AI) research and logical reasoning concerning the intentions and beliefs of the speakers. For instance, the Cohen and Levesque model (Cohen and Levesque 1990a, 1990b) postulates communication as teamwork between rational agents that are committed to their individual persistent goals as well as their mutually believed joint persistent goals. The goals are "persistent" in that the agents are committed to them and keep trying to achieve them unless trying is no longer rational. Cohen and Levesque define commitments to the individual and joint goals slightly differently thus catching the difference between one's own intention and those agreed between the partners. With the joint goals, in particular, the agents are required to communicate with others if the prerequisites of the commitment do not hold anymore, that is, if some of the preconditions of the joint goal are fulfilled, or if the joint goal has been reached. Concerning the individual goals, communication is not necessary about their status although in some cases this may be expected as part of socially fluent behaviour. In the SharedPlan approach, however, Grosz and Sidner (1990) postulate joint intentions among agents who are engaged in collaboration by building and sharing a plan. The agents plan their actions using joint intentions in the same manner as they do with their individual intentions, and the joint and individual intentions do not differ from each other in this respect. The difference between the two models for collaboration seems to lie in the different aspects of communication that they deal with: whereas the Cohen and Levesque model focuses mainly on logical reasoning and communication, the SharedPlan model emphasises that it is not enough to just communicate the changed plan to the partner but the whole planning needs to be stopped as well. The SharedPlan model has been further developed in dialogue systems, including planning interleaved with the dialogue structure (Lochaum, 1994) and integration of the model into Collagen, a collaborative interface agent framework (Sidner et al., 2000; Rich et al. 2005).

Collaboration is also studied in conversational settings in relation to feedback and turn-taking processes: it is pointed out that the interlocutors take turns and give feedback to their partners, either in verbal or nonverbal form, so as to coordinate their interaction and build shared knowledge. The grounding model (Clark and Wilkes-Gibbs, 1986) postulates that the dialogue consists of a cycle of presentation and acceptance phases whereby the agent presents information to the partner, and the partner evaluates the relevance and acceptability of the presented information within the current context and the partner's individual intentions. Cooperation is based on the agents' need to communicate with each other if they have understood the previous message and how it fits in with their own goals and intentions so as to be able to work together towards the shared goals. Traum (1996, 1999) introduces specific grounding acts that the agents use for building mutual understanding of the dialogue, whereas Jokinen (1996) considers the agents' commitment based on conforming to general rules of coordination and cooperation.

Recently, cognitively oriented research has also focused on the speakers' cooperation and adaptation to each other's behavior. This type of behavior is called alignment (Pickering and Garrod, 2004), and it is assumed to take place on different linguistic levels, starting from phonetic adaptation to words and utterance level adaptation. Alignment has been the focus of many investigations concerning subtle nonverbal cues that indicate the interlocutors' willingness to cooperate with their partner in turn-taking, feedback giving processes, and information structuring in dialogues.

Another view of cooperation is provided by Allwood (1976), who examines cooperation in a larger context of coordinated human communication in general (see an overview of the approach e.g. in Allwood et al., 2001). Communicative Activity Analysis regards communication as a motivated rational activity, coordinated through communicative obligations and the basic assumptions of Ideal Cooperation. The speakers are engaged in Ideal Cooperation, if they

1. Have a joint purpose
2. Consider each other cognitively
3. Consider each other ethically
4. Trust each other to follow the same principles of items (1)–(3).

The distinctive feature in this definition is the emphasis on the social obligations between the agents: interlocutors assume that their partners take into account the ethical aspects of cooperation (i.e., their actions are not based on efficiency and effectiveness only, but also follow some ethical considerations), and the fundamental role of trust. Trust refers to the speakers' assumptions that their partner will behave in a rational manner and in accordance with general communicative principles.

Trust is not just a belief in the partner's benevolent intentions, but a matter of observing the partner's behaviour in attempting to achieve the joint goal. In this, not only verbal communication but also non-verbal signals are important cues for building trust and creating an image of a trustworthy partner. Cooperation emerges from this shared activity, and as long as the assumptions of Ideal Cooperation hold, the partner is regarded as a rational interlocutor, willing to continue communication and act in order to achieve the shared dialogue goals. If the assumptions are not fulfilled (although the agent seems to perceive and understand the partner's contributions), the partner's behavior is regarded as uncooperative, lacking the basic willingness to communicate and to react in an appropriate manner. If the assumptions of Ideal Cooperation do not hold at all, the situation can develop into a conflict, and if the conflict becomes so serious that it makes any cooperation impossible, communication will break down as well.

The Constructive Dialogue Modelling approach (CDM; Jokinen, 2009) implements some of the assumptions of Allwood's Ideal Communication. CDM is an AI-based approach to interaction management, where communicative behavior is based on the rational agents' observations about the world and on their reasoning, within the dialogue context, about the new information that is being exchanged in dialogue contributions. In CDM, communication is regarded as a fundamentally cooperative activity whereby the agents construct mutual understanding of how to resolve the underlying task. The agents construct a shared model of how to achieve their goals, which they have independently set for themselves, to accomplish some real-world task (e.g., rent a car, assemble a pump, book a flight, find their way) or just to keep the channel open. The agents must communicate with each other about their intentions in order to tell their partners about their goals as well as to obtain and provide necessary information related to the goals. The agents' actions are constrained by communicative obligations arising from the particular activity they are engaged in and have a certain role in, and this activity creates cooperation among the dialogue partners who try to fulfill the goals set for the dialogue. In CDM, attention is paid to the planning and generation of appropriate responses, since the success of interaction depends on the cognitive and emotional impact of the response on the hearer.

In summary, system requirements that deal with cooperation and address the user's communicative needs are important for the design and development of spoken dialogue systems. Gibbon et al. (2000) talk about the "contextual appropriateness" of the system, which includes Grice's cooperation maxims and adaptation, whereas Dybkjaer et al. (1997) provide a set of best-practice recommendations based on the Gricean maxims. In the ubiquitous and mobile computing context, the requirement of trust has also become important (e.g. Kaasinen, 2005). In this context, trust refers to the user's trust in the service provider and is an indicator of a positive belief or expectation of the future service based on the previous performance. One of the main questions to investigate is to determine the conditions and requirements for creating, supporting and losing trust concerning reliable services and information. In these studies, the development of trust and cooperation in human communication may provide useful reference points.

Cooperation and communicative competence are usually related to the speaker's ability to recognize the partner's interaction strategies and preferences and to draw appropriate conclusions of how to continue the interaction. As interactive systems become more conversational, cooperation also becomes more dynamic and does not appear only as a particular means to guarantee comprehensibility of individual utterances or effective communication, but as an effect that emerges from the dialogue partners' willingness to continue communication and make relevant contributions until the communicative goals have been achieved and the partners are satisfied with the result. In other words, perceived cooperation supports trust and reliable communication. Jokinen (2009) summarizes the communicative competence of spoken dialogue systems in the following four requirements:

1. The system must have an adequate and physically feasible interface. This is related to the enablement of successful interaction, the transparency of the system's functionality, input/output modalities, voice quality, etc.
2. The system must have efficient reasoning components. This deals with fast algorithms and architectures that support efficient and flexible system performance.
3. The system must support natural language robustness. This concerns the system's linguistic competence, including nonverbal communication, which is necessary for the interpretation and generation of utterances.
4. The system must be conversationally adequate. This includes pragmatic aspects of interaction that contribute to cooperative communication, such as the ability to select appropriate dialogue strategies to get a message across; to give feedback to clarify vagueness and clear up possible confusion, misunderstanding, or lack of understanding; and to adapt to the user's preferences and interaction styles as necessary.

5.2   ADAPTATION AND USER MODELLING

Besides the dialogue management model that deals with the system's conversational capability, it is also useful to have a separate user modelling component that records the system's knowledge of the user's characteristics as well as maintaining a model of the user's beliefs and of the system's beliefs. User modelling has been studied from early on in AI-based dialogue management since the knowledge of the user's beliefs and intentions is important for planning reactions to the user's input: system responses are based on the system's reasoning with respect to what the user may already know and what the user may want to know through the dialogue (Kobsa and Wahlster, 1989). Much of the User Modelling work has focused on logic and AI-based belief modelling, updating the speakers' knowledge base, and dealing with contradictory or partial information in the reasoning.

In present-day dialogue applications, user modelling is often limited to a simple listing of user preferences concerning various interface properties. AI-based user modelling becomes relevant in negotiation or planning dialogues, where the system needs to maintain the user's beliefs, and in selecting suitable interaction strategies for clearing misunderstandings. Plan-based dialogue systems (see Section 4.2) have extensive user modelling components that record the system's knowledge of the user's beliefs and characteristics, and allow the system to address specific user properties when planning its responses. In statistical dialogue systems, the term user modelling has also been used, but in quite a different manner: it refers to an automated dialogue partner that simulates the role of an unknown "user" and provides systematically varied inputs to test implemented dialogue control strategies and to enable the acquisition of a corpus of dialogues. In this work, the model of the simulated user is often referred to as the user model (see Section 2.4).

User modelling also concerns user profiling and adaptation, that is, tailoring the interaction with respect to the user's preferences. This is common in e-commerce and with various types of information providers (news filtering, TV programs guides, book, or web browsing recommendations) that can thus provide personalized access to information sources. In this context, user profiles enable preferred filtering and rating of incoming information. They can be produced by letting the user explicitly specify their preferences in a user profile database, or by monitoring the user's interactions with the system, for example, their navigation choices or a list of specific keywords in their search queries. Users may also give explicit feedback about the system's recommendations and thus teach the system about their interests over time. Besides individual profiling, information about groups of users may also be exploited in the profiles. Collaborative filtering is commonly used in recommender systems (Goldberg et al., 1992), where the preference information of a user group is tracked by comparing the statistical similarity of the selected items of one user with the items selected by another user.

In dialogue management, user modelling and adaptation are generally considered properties of an interactive system that facilitate more effective and natural interaction. User Models can support the dialogue manager in selecting interaction strategies and presentation techniques that allow smooth communication and help the user to "feel at ease." For instance, knowledge of the words and phrases that are commonly used by the user can be deployed when presenting information to the user, as well as to build expectations about the user's utterances and to restrict the speech recognizer's vocabulary to provide better recognition. Also, the system's adaptation to take the initiative depending on the dialogue situation can be used to overcome problematic error situations. Adaptation has thus been widely investigated in order to remedy communication disfluencies (Danieli and Gerbino, 1995; Krahmer et al., 1999; Walker et al., 2000a, 2000b; Litman and Pan, 2002) and to monitor the user's familiarity with the system functionality (novice vs. expert) so as to tailor system prompts according to the user's skills (Paris, 1988; Yankelovich, 1996; Jokinen and Kanto, 2004).

On the system design level, there are several issues that make adaptation complex. One of the main issues is to decide who is in control of adaptation: the user or the system. Smith (1993) already observed that it is safer for beginners to be closely guided by the system, whereas experienced users usually like to take the initiative, which also results in more efficient dialogues in terms of decreased average completion time and decreased average number of utterances. A related question concerns the direction of adaptation, that is, who needs to adapt to what and when. The usual case has been user adaptation, that is, the user learns system properties and functionalities, due to human superiority in adapting to different situations. If the system is to adapt to the user, the system needs to be equipped with the architecture that supports adaptive functionality as well as with models of possible user behaviour. However, full adaptation capability deals with the user's habits and preferences, attitudes and intentions, temperament, and style, some of which is difficult if not next to impossible to model to the level of the required accuracy.

Concerning usability of adaptive systems, we also encounter questions such as the desirability of adaptation. It has been strongly argued that adaptation is not desirable since it confuses the user concerning the system's functionality, and can even hinder the user from accomplishing her task (Shneiderman, 1998). In general, usability studies emphasise the importance of the users having the feeling that they are in control of all the application properties. Thus system adaptation should also follow some comprehensible patterns that the users can follow, since unsolicited adaptation may result in confusion and ultimately decrease user satisfaction. One solution is to give the user an explicit option to change the system's interface and interaction properties, for example, swap between different input modalities or switch between system-initiative and user-initiative dialogue strategies depending on the situation (Litman and Pan, 2002). This makes the system more transparent, and apparently also adds to user satisfaction as the user can feel in control of the system. On the other hand, there is also evidence that users may not want to take the initiative even if given such a possibility: Jameson and Schwarzkopf (2002) studied users interacting with an adaptive recommendation system for the Web, and observed that although letting the user decide the moment of adaptation may indeed enhance the feeling of control, users were not necessarily interested in using this facility.

However, if the system is regarded as a conversational agent, adaptation to the user can actually become one of the desirable features of the system because it can support the user's accomplishment of a task by providing appropriate and contextually relevant information. Adaptation can also allow friendlier interaction, since the system in a certain manner "understands" the user and can pick up relevant and interesting topics for the user's attention. This type of adaptation is relevant in order to create and maintain rapport between the system and the user: the user can feel that the system "listens" and "understands" his/her particular needs.

5.3   MULTIMODALITY

Natural language communication is intrinsically multimodal: we receive visual, auditory, tactile, etc., data through our sensory system, process it further in our cognitive system, and use the changes in our cognitive state as a starting point to perform actions in order to react and coordinate our environment. In human–computer interactions, multimodality thus offers a natural way to expand the interaction capabilities of spoken dialogue systems and provide users with more flexible and enjoyable interfaces. Naturally, realistic usage situations for multimodal systems require more complicated tasks than typical information-seeking tasks so as to provide extra value of the new modality to the user. This also requires extended natural language processing capability and/or interactive situations where a unimodal interface does not seem appropriate. It must be emphasized that multimodality is also important in supporting universal access to digital information and allowing users with special needs to gain opportunities for communication and interaction (see, e.g., Stephanidis, 2009). In these cases, multimodality not only extends the application's versatility and robustness, but in fact functions as the only possible way to interface with the user.

In human communication, the term *modality* is used to refer to the various sensory systems through which incoming data are transformed to higher-level representations, or the intended messages are translated into outgoing data expressions in speech and movements. In human–computer interaction, modality is understood as a computer subsystem that corresponds to the use of human sensory channels, with the various input/output devices analogous to sensory organs. For instance, Nigay and Coutaz (1995) emphasize the system-oriented aspects of their definitions: modality refers to the type of communication channel used to convey information. Distinction is also made between the devices through which information is received and transmitted (camera, graphical displays, loudspeakers, vibrating mouse, etc.) and the encoding of data in different media using different coding systems. For instance, computer displays can show text, graphics, and video, all of which are transmitted through the visual modality, but use different coding systems to present the information.

A typical multimodal interaction is given below and in Figure 5.1 (from Jokinen, 2009). The system provides information about public transportation and helps the user to navigate from a departure point to a destination. The interaction modalities are speech and a touchpad interface.

U: Uh, how do I get from the Railway station . . . uh.
S: *Where was it you wanted to go?*
U: Well, there! + <map gesture>
S: *Wait as I retrieve the information. Tram 3B leaves Railway Station at 14:40, there is one change. Arrival time at Brahe Street 7 is 14:57.*
U: When does the next one go?
S: *Wait as I retrieve the information. Bus 23 leaves Railway Station at 14:43, there are no changes. Arrival time at Brahe Street 7 is 15:02.*

The user can specify important concepts such as the departure and arrival locations by speaking and also by tapping the touchscreen. If the user draws a circle instead of pointing to a single point, the whole area is taken as the focus where available public transportation is considered to be

FIGURE 5.1: Tactile input at left and a graphical representation of a route at right (from Jokinen, 2009).

found. The system can respond in speech and also by drawing a route on the map. In this particular case, a verbal route description is also available if the user prefers to read written text rather than listen to the speech.

The information in the different input and output modality channels can have different relations with respect to each other depending on how the main message is encoded into the modalities (see Martin, 1997). For instance, two pieces of information in the different modalities can complement each other if they contribute toward the same meaning but could not be interpreted in a meaningful way as stand-alone unimodality expressions (e.g., if one points to a location and says simultaneously "well, there!"). They can also be redundant if the same information is conveyed in both modalities independently (e.g., blinking the element on the map at the point that denotes railway station and uttering simultaneously: "Tram 3B leaves Railway Station"). The information items in the different channels can also contradict each other, for example, if one circles a location and says simultaneously "this bus stop here" but the circle does not contain any references to bus stops (this is, of course, not reasonable as a system output but may occur as a user input). However, much research is still needed to fully understand how the different modalities complement and contradict each other in order to make the information presentation effective, and how to interpret imprecise information (see, e.g., Choumane and Siroux, 2007). Moreover, it is also important to study how humans perceive the various signals transmitted through the different modality channels as important and effective messages.

Besides the interpretation of multimodal signals, another main question in multimodal system design is the appropriate level of fusion and fission of the information in the modality channels. The fusion of information refers to the analysis and integration of input information that arrives through the different modalities into a composite input, i.e. to a meaningful communicative act, whereas the fission of information is the opposite process at the generation side and refers to the division of information into appropriate modalities so as to generate an efficient presentation to the user.

Nigay and Coutaz (1995) (cf. also Gibbon et al., 2000) identified three levels of fusion: lexical, syntactic, and semantic. Lexical fusion happens on the hardware and software levels, for example, when selecting objects with the shift key down. The syntactic fusion involves combining data to form a syntactically complete command, whereas semantic fusion concerns the detailed functionality of the interface and defines the meanings of the actions. Usually, semantic fusion takes place on two levels: in the first phase inputs are combined into events, and those events that belong to the predefined set of multimodal input events are picked up. In the second phase, the events are handed over to the higher-level interpreter, which uses its knowledge about the user's intentions and the context to finalize and disambiguate the input. For instance, in the case of multimodal language communication, the concepts and meanings are extracted from the different modalities (speech, touch, etc.), and the data are combined to produce a single meaning representation for the user's action. Multimodal fusion on the linguistic level is described in more detailed e.g. by Johnston (1998), who uses a unification framework to build a coherent and consistent interpretation of the different modality sources. In the MUMS system (MUlti-Modal navigation System) (Hurtig and Jokinen, 2006), the example system shown above, fusion corresponds to three operations that take care of the production of legal combinations, weighting of possible combinations, and selection of the best candidate, as schematically shown in Figure 5.2.

On the architectural level, efficiency of the fusion and fission components plays an important role in guaranteeing reasonable functioning of the system. Nigay and Coutaz (1995) present a fusion architecture called PAC Amodeus, which supports concurrent signal processing, whereas agent-based architectures, such as Open Agent Architecture, have a special multimodality coordination agent that produces a single meaning from multiple input modalities aiming at matching this with the user's intentions. The W3C working group for Multimodal Interaction (http://mojo .w3.org/2002/mmi/) focuses on the architecture for multimodal user interfaces in order to provide a framework for integrating different modalities such as speech, handwriting, and keystrokes especially for Web-based multimodal applications. The group works on flexible interaction possi-

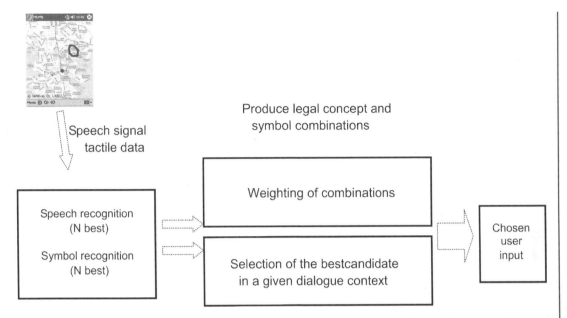

FIGURE 5.2: Graphical presentation of the MUMS multimodal fusion (from Hurtig and Jokinen, 2006).

bilities and solutions for mobile, in-car, and home applications, and has produced the Multimodal Interaction Framework (http://mojo.w3.org/TR/mmi-framework/), which is a general architecture specification identifying markup languages, major components, as well as input and output modes for multimodal systems.

The Multimodal Interaction working group has also developed a representation language Extensible Multi-Modal Annotations (EMMA), which is an Extensible Markup Language-based data exchange format for the interface between input processors and interaction management systems. The interpretation of the user's input is generated by signal interpretation processes, such as speech and ink recognition and semantic interpreters, and it is expected to be used by other components that manipulate the user's inputs further, such as interaction and dialogue managers. For instance, the interpretation of a user input, derived from a speech, pen, or keystroke signal, is its transcription into words, whereas the meaning of an utterance or an accompanying gesture can be described as a set of attribute/value pairs. An example of the EMMA representation is given below, where an interpretation of the user contribution "put this battleship here" contains a speech input (the element identified as `int1` with the features `medium=acoustic` and `mode=speech` in `emma:interpretation`) and a sequence of two pen gestures (the elements identified as `int2` and `int3` in `emma:sequence`) (the example is from the EMMA website).

```
<emma:emma version="1.0"
    xmlns:emma:="http://www.w3.org/2003/04/emma"
    xmlns:xsi="http://www.w3.org/2001/XMLSchema-instance"
    xsi:schemaLocation="http://www.w3.org/2003/04/emma
    http://www.w3.org/TR/emma/emma10.xsd"
    xmlns="http://www.example.com/example">
<emma:group id="grp">
<emma:interpretation id="int1" emma:medium="acoustic"
emma:mode="speech">
    <action>move</action>
    <object>this-battleship</object>
    <destination>here</destination>
</emma:interpretation>
<emma:sequence id="seq1">
    <emma:interpretation id="int2" emma:medium="tactile"
emma:mode="ink">
        <x>0.253</x>
         <y>0.124</y>
    </emma:interpretation>
    <emma:interpretation id="int3" emma:medium="tactile"
emma:mode="ink">
        <x>0.866</x>
        <y>0.724</y>
    </emma:interpretation>
</emma:sequence>
</emma:group>
</emma:emma>
```

One of the first multimodal system is considered to be Bolt's *Put that there* system (Bolt, 1980), which allowed users to interact with the world using speech and pointing gestures on the projection of the world on the wall. Many systems have since been developed, usually with pen and speech interfaces, but also with fairly rich interaction capabilities: for instance, the TravelMate system (Cheyer and Julia, 1995) is an agent-based multimodal map application, which also has access to WWW sources, and has also been extended to augmented reality. The input can be handwritten text, gestures, speech, and direct manipulation commands, and output can be textual, graphical, audio, and video data. In the SmartKom project (Wahlster, 2006), technologies for speech, gesture, and graphics were combined into a large system and the interaction with the system took place via a lifelike character Smartakus. The architecture was aimed at general applicability, and was demonstrated on three different application situations: public information kiosk, home infotainment, and mobile travel companion. Multimodal interactive systems can also be related to edutainment, where the interaction is meant to be entertaining while providing useful information (e.g., the Hans Christian Andersen system; Bernsen et al., 2004). As mentioned above, multimodal applications are especially suitable for tasks requiring rich communicative possibilities and interactive situations that would be cumbersome or not possible at all with a unimodal interface. Many practical applications concern location-based services and tasks where spatial information is referred to, such as map navigation and way-finding applications for which multimodality offers a natural interface. Novel applications are also brought in through robotics and the robot's interaction with human users (Bos et al., 2003; Bennewitz et al., 2007; Kruijff et al. 2008), and the gesture and face recognition technology allows communication to take place besides speech also through gestures and facial expressions.

5.4   NATURAL INTERACTION

Another line of dialogue research deals with natural interaction. Although the concept of naturalness is rather a vague concept, in relation to spoken dialogue systems it is often used to refer to intuitive interfaces that allow users to interact effortlessly and in a manner that they find most suitable for the task at hand. Jokinen (2009) talks about dialogue systems with natural language capability as affordable interfaces to the digital world. In interface design, the term "affordable" has been used to refer to an interface that readily suggests to the user appropriate ways in which it can be used, and in the case of spoken dialogue systems, we can use it to describe the system as an interface that should lend itself to natural interaction without the users needing to think how the communication should take place in order to get the task completed.

In designing multimodal spoken dialogue systems and considering the intuitive, affordable aspects of input and output possibilities, it is necessary to increase our understanding of how the modalities are used in communication in general. This leads to investigations on nonverbal and multimodal communication among humans, and building systems that take these new modalities into account. Much of this type of research is done within the Embodied Conversational Agents and immersive conversational environments (Cassel et al., 2003; Traum et al., 2007; André and Pelachaud, 2009). These agents are built to model characteristics of human–human interaction so as to investigate hypotheses of how communication takes place on one hand, and to develop natural communication possibilities for humans interacting with artificial characters on the other hand. The work has especially focused on nonverbal communication behavior such as gaze and gesturing in dialogue management, and on social structures and relations among groups of agents. Through the analysis of interactions between humans, a better understanding of the conversational activity, attentional state, as well as the sources for rapport, joy, excitement, etc., can be achieved, and it is expected that models for these aspects of communication will improve robustness in communication between humans and intelligent agents.

Much effort has also been devoted to corpus collection for technology development and to annotation of multimodal corpora so as to provide analyzed data for experimental studies on natural human interactions. Such projects as AMI (Augmented Multi-party Interaction) (http://www.amiproject.org/) and CALO (Cognitive Assistant that Learns and Organizes) have collected multimodal corpora in the context of multiparty meeting settings and aimed at developing technology that will augment communication between individuals and groups of people. Many smaller cooperation projects have focused on free-flowing conversations and e.g. in MUMIN (Multimodal Interaction) (www.cst.dk/mumin) a particular annotation scheme has been developed for general behaviours such as feedback and turn-taking processing using gestures, facial expressions, and body posture.

5.5   SUMMARY

This chapter has discussed selected topics in advanced dialogue management, and focused especially on cooperation, adaptation, multimodality, and natural interaction. These topics were singled out because they include interaction modelling that goes beyond task-oriented applications and they also take dialogue systems toward more conversational systems that users may enjoy interacting with.

In future visions of ubiquitous computing (Weiser, 1991), interactive systems are embedded in the environment, and everyday communication may include communication with systems that converse with humans using natural language. As technology development allows our environment to become more sensitive to various human activities, for example, detecting people's faces and movements in a room as well as observing social communication patterns, it is possible that computer systems will also learn natural human communication patterns and strategies that are typical for humans. This leads to situations where it may be difficult to describe dialogue systems in a traditional manner as interactive interfaces between the user and the database, but a new metaphor is needed that regards interactions between the user and the system as communicative situations between agents (Jokinen, 2009). Although much of this metaphor is still under active research, there is also support for the view that the users do not necessarily consider dialogue systems as tools but as interactive partners that they interact with. For instance, Reeves and Nass (1996) argued that users equate media and real life, and assign humanlike properties to computers, so that they treat them (and other media) as agents with which interaction is based on human social and natural habits.

CHAPTER 6

Methodologies and Practices of Evaluation

In this chapter, we focus on the evaluation of dialogue systems. We first present a short historical overview of the evaluation task in Section 6.1, and then discuss some concepts and definitions of evaluation approaches and data collection in Section 6.2. We then introduce different evaluation metrics in Section 6.3, and evaluation frameworks in Section 6.4. We also discuss usability evaluation in Section 6.5, and two specific topics of evaluation in Section 6.6: semiautomatic evaluation and standardization. We conclude the chapter with challenges introduced by multimodal and conversational dialogue systems in Section 6.7.

6.1 HISTORICAL OVERVIEW

Large-scale evaluation became a more prominent topic in the late 1980s, when ARPA/DARPA (Defense Advanced Research Project Agency) started competitive projects to assess the development of speech technology. Research initiatives consisted of building shared speech databases for the development of speech recognizers and of comparing the performance of different systems on predefined tasks. For instance, the Resource Management task (Price et al., 1988) dealt with digits and isolated words, and later the ATIS project (Price, 1990) with full sentences and read speech. The assessment exercise was also extended to interaction technology, with the Switchboard corpus (Jurafsky et al., 1997) focusing on the collection and annotation of natural telephone conversations, and the Communicator project (http://communicator.sourceforge.net/; Walker et al., 2002) on the construction and evaluation of spoken dialogue systems.

Similar initiatives were also put forward in Europe, although the emphasis was more on collaborative projects than competition. Much of the evaluation work was directed toward formulation of standards, and early efforts in this respect were coordinated by the EAGLES (Expert Advisory Group on Language Engineering Standards) project (King et al., 1996). The project produced a thorough overview of systems and techniques in language engineering, of which dialogue and discourse processing was a subfield, in the form of the EAGLES Handbook (Cole et al., 1997). Part 2 of the handbook (Gibbon et al., 2000) gives a more technical overview of the state-of-the-art technology. In the European R&D frameworks, other projects also worked on assessing state-of-the-art speech and language engineering. For instance, the SQALE (Speech Recognizer Quality Assessment in Language Engineering) project (Young et al., 1997) carried out assessment of large vocabulary, continuous speech recognition systems in a multilingual environment, and the DISC project (Spoken Language Dialogue Systems and Components: Best practice in development and evaluation) (Bernsen and Dybkjær, 1997) surveyed spoken language dialogue systems. The CLASS project (Collaboration in Language and Speech Science and technology) (Jacquemin et al., 2000) also included speech and language technology assessment and organized a special evaluation workshop at the LREC 2000 conference (Language Resources and Evaluation Conference). The continuation of the EAGLES initiative was the ISLE project (International Standards for Language Engineering), which aimed at coordinating activities in the field of Human Language Technology (HLT), and worked in collaboration with some U.S. partners within the EU–US International Research Cooperation Initiative. The ISLE project consisted of subgroups such as the multilingual lexicons subgroup, the natural interaction and multimodality (NIMM) subgroup, and the evaluation of HLT systems subgroup, and the goal of the working groups was to prepare, develop, and promote standards and recommendations for language resources, tools, and products. The NIMM subgroup surveyed best-practice techniques and technology for (multimodal) dialogue corpus collection, annotation, and system development (Bernsen and Dybkjær, 2002).

Nowadays, assessments of the performance of spoken dialogue systems is a standard part of the development of dialogue systems, and can also include usability evaluations, although extensive usability testing with real users in real situations is usually done only in companies and industrial environments with prospective products. General methodology and metrics are still research issues, but guidelines and recommendations of best practices are provided in large-scale industrial standardization work, such as is conducted within the ISO (International Organization for Standardization) groups and the World Wide Web Consortium (W3C). Effort has also been directed toward different evaluation challenges and toward the building of shared infrastructure, corpora, and open-source system components that allow rapid prototyping and development of systems, and can also function as a basis for teaching and training. On the other hand, development of more complex and advanced dialogue systems has also introduced evaluation challenges involving issues such as the evaluation of multimodality and the system's naturalness and conversational capability. Also comparison and prediction of system properties across different tasks and users have become important, especially in industrial applications where the usability issues are crucial. Another line of research has dealt with automatic evaluation and user simulations in order to enable quick assessment of design ideas without resource-consuming corpus collection and user studies. This type of evaluation exercise usually focuses on the properties of statistical and machine learning techniques, with the goal of assessing the quality of different dialogue strategies, and comparing the appropriateness of the methods and metrics that are used in optimizing these strategies.

6.2   SOME DISTINCTIONS AND DEFINITIONS

6.2.1   Evaluation Approaches and Data Collection

One of the main discussion points in dialogue system development and evaluation deals with whether to conduct evaluation in laboratory or field conditions. The difference concerns the reality of the evaluation conditions: under laboratory conditions, the tests take place in the development environment or in a particular usability laboratory, whereas field testing refers to observations of the users using the system as part of their normal activities in actual situations.

Real situations are generally regarded as providing the best conditions for collecting data, but in practise, laboratory evaluations are often the preferred form of evaluation, since evaluation in real or almost real situations is costly due to the complexity of the evaluation setup. Free-flowing situations may also cause unexpected results that may be avoided under controlled situations because of the possibility for parametric and systematic evaluation of the system. However, laboratory evaluations do not necessarily reflect the difficult conditions in which the system would be used in reality: task descriptions and user requirements may be unrepresentative of some situations that occur in authentic usage contexts, and the controlled illumination, noise, mobility, etc., create clean test conditions. Results from the evaluations in this kind of idealized conditions are thus understood as showing the upper bound limits of the system or component operation.

A more serious problem in laboratory evaluations is the fact that the subjects adapt themselves to the given scenario. Evaluations of practical systems has recently shown differences in the users' performance, depending on whether the users are motivated by an extrinsic goal to use the system or if they just participate in an experiment (Rudnicky et al., 2000). The subjects only participating in the experiment try to behave as if they were in a real situation, and thus, instead of exhibiting real behaviour, they act (more or less consciously) according to the expectations they have about the scenario. Ai et al. (2007) systematically compared acted and motivated interactions using two corpora, one of which contained acted interactions with the system under laboratory situations, and the other interactions with the system in public use with users who possibly had a genuine reason to use the system. They noticed, for instance, that the real users asked for help and used barge-in more frequently than the recruited subjects, who talked more and faster with the system than the real users. Interactions also differed in the number and types of dialogue acts used, but not in the distribution of the acts, which suggests that the overall structure of the dialogues is the same although the users may have different needs for the means of interaction, as exhibited by the high rate of help requests and barge-ins by the real users.

Besides the distinction between real and laboratory conditions for evaluation, we can also talk about distinction between empirical and theoretical approaches to evaluation. This is related to the evaluator's assumptions about the users, system parameters, and context, and how these may influence the system performance. Some theoretical assumptions are always involved in system design and evaluation, so the line between the two approaches is actually a scale from techniques with weak theoretical assumptions to those based on strong claims of the nature of the evaluation objects. The more theoretically oriented setups typically aim at verifying the consistency of a certain model or at assessing predictions that the model makes about the application domain, whereas the less theoretical approaches tend to collect data on the basis of which empirical models can be compared and elaborated.

Both approaches can be combined with evaluations conducted in laboratory or real usage conditions. We can talk about controlled or free user studies depending on how strong are the theoretical assumptions that are used to control the evaluation conditions, and we can talk about real or simulated evaluations depending on how realistic the evaluation conditions are. Table 6.1 summarizes the different evaluation approaches with respect to testing conditions and assumptions. The types form a rough clustering rather than a clear-cut classification of the different alternatives, but they can help to clarify the impact of underlying assumptions on the evaluation in general.

While user and system simulations can be semiautomated, controlled user studies require carefully balanced collection of users in the particular test environment, where an attempt is made to keep the unnecessary or irrelevant aspects of the situation as stable as possible. If the users' behaviour is minimally or not at all constrained, the approach in real conditions amounts to free user studies, while in laboratory conditions this is often referred to as Wizard of Oz (WOZ) experiments. In WOZ experiments, the system is totally or partially simulated by a human wizard, and the goal is to obtain information about the users' behaviour in cases where the planned system does not yet exist, or only some parts of the system exist. WOZ studies have been a rather popular method in data collection and in the preliminary evaluation of dialogue systems, but their use has diminished partly due to the preference for "real user" data as the empirical basis for modeling interactions, and partly due to automated laboratory evaluations of system components. Because of the requirement for real subjects, WOZ studies are not necessarily a cheap and quick way to test the system's dialogue strategies, and it also takes time to train the wizard to behave in a consistent manner. Moreover, the wizard's human reasoning capability may affect the consistency and "system-likeness" of the behaviour of the same wizard, and across several wizards.

TABLE 6.1: Different evaluation assumptions and conditions.		
	LABORATORY CONDITIONS	**REAL USAGE CONDITIONS**
Weak theoretical assumptions	Wizard of Oz simulations	Free user studies
Strong theoretical assumptions	User and system simulations	Controlled user studies

When developing practical applications for real usage, it is necessary to take the users' needs and requirements into account in the early stages of the development process, rather than delay user evaluation to a later phase of the project when it is more difficult if not impossible to take the user's view-points into consideration. In the user-centred design approach, the users are invited to take part in the system design and development from the very beginning, so as to provide data of the user's wishes and views as well to test system versions on real users. In software development, the same idea is related to the iterative development approach that intertwines system building with testing and evaluation of the components in an incremental manner.

6.2.2   Evaluation Goals and Types of Evaluation

One of the first steps in setting up an evaluation task is to clarify the goals. The evaluator may be interested in the user's views and perception of the system, the naturalness of interaction, functioning of a particular component or the system as a whole, comparison of the system (component) with another system, or finding out how much the system performance has improved since its previous version.

Depending on the goals, different types of evaluation can be distinguished. Hirschman and Thompson (1997) define three types of evaluation: performance evaluation (to assess if the system's goals are achieved in an efficient manner), diagnostic evaluation (to produce a system's performance profile), and adequacy evaluation (to determine the fitness of a system for a specific purpose). Möller (2002, 2005a), however, refers to the above-mentioned performance and adequacy evaluations as assessment, and introduces a new type of evaluation, quality of experience (QoE), which concerns the user's experience of the system use (see more in Section 6.52.). In the discussion below, we deal with evaluation types based on the different notions of appropriateness that dialogue systems can exhibit:

1. Functional evaluation—Is the system functionally appropriate?
2. Performance evaluation—How well does the system perform on the particular task it is designed for?
3. Usability and quality evaluation—Are the potential and real users satisfied with the system's performance, and how do the users perceive the system when using it?
4. Reusability evaluation—Is the system flexible and portable?

The goals of functional evaluation are related to the system's initial requirements. The system is built for a particular task and with a particular application in mind, and functional evaluation seeks to pin down if and how the system fulfills the requirements set for its development. The criteria for functional evaluation are set in the system's design phase when the system and task requirements are defined in the context of potential users, and they are later used to assess how well the complete system meets the original requirements. Functional evaluation concerns the system's *usefulness* for a particular task, thus comparing what the system is meant to do and what it actually does, and measuring the appropriateness of the different components and algorithms in supporting the overall functionality of the system.

Performance evaluation concerns the system's efficiency and robustness in achieving the task goals, and can focus on the whole system or one of its components. Performance is assessed with respect to the criteria set forth in the evaluation goals and usually presupposes a well-defined baseline against which the system performance can be compared. In diagnostic-type evaluations, a representative test suite is used so as to produce a system's performance profile with respect to a taxonomy of possible inputs. Concerning industrial applications offering services for users (information search, reservations, guidance, etc.), performance evaluation also deals with the quality of the service offered by the system. This concerns issues such as service support, service operability, serveability, and service security (cf. quality of service definition in ITU-T Rec. E.800, 1994). The evaluation also needs to address the question of how the system performs in real situations where hundreds of users want to use the system simultaneously with different but genuine needs. Performance evaluation is typically done by system developers who want to compare alternative implementations of a technology, or to evaluate progress in successive generations of the same implementation. It has also been called progressive evaluation, summative evaluation, calibration, and diagnostics.

When the focus of the evaluation is on the user and the user's needs, we talk about usability evaluation. The main question is if, from the user's perspective, the system is *usable* for the particular task, and if the users can achieve their goals in the manner they expect to. Usability is measured through the users' subjective views of the success of the interaction, and an important criterion is the user's satisfaction with the system. Usability testing is usually done by usability experts who observe users using the system. They consider e.g. what the users like and dislike, what they need, how well the system supports the users in the particular task, and what type of cognitive mismatches there may be between the user's and the designer's understanding of how the system works. In human–computer interaction (HCI), usability testing is thus considered a process of learning from the users what a usable system is, and different techniques combine observations of the users using the system with user interviews and questionnaires.

The users' evaluations of the system are strongly related to what they expect from the system and how they perceive the system as fulfilling its function. If the evaluation is based on the users' perceptions of the system, we can talk about the (perceived) quality of the system and measure it through the selection of certain quality aspects that the users' evaluation is focused on. Some of the main questions that the quality evaluation tries to answer in this respect are: what extra value does the system bring to the user in regard to task completion and does the interaction create trust and acceptance in the user.

Finally, an important question from the point of view of system development concerns the system's *reusability*. This can be measured by linking it to the issues of how easy it is to maintain and upgrade the system. System developers may also find it useful to know if it is possible to use the system, or parts of it, when building a new system or extending the old system's functionality to new domains, new tasks, and new applications. A modular and extendable system architecture supports these goals, and thus portability and multifunctionality can be assessed together with the system's other technical properties. They are also related to the financial aspects of research and development of spoken dialogue systems, especially in industrial contexts and for commercial purposes. Issues dealing with open-source architectures and licensing may also become important factors in this context. From the user's point of view, reusability can be linked to the easy use and learning of the system's functionalities.

6.3   EVALUATION MEASURES

An important question in operationalizing the evaluation is what type of measurements to use to quantify the evaluation goal. The indicators should be indicative of the goal they aim at measuring, independent of each other, and preferably on such a general level that they can be applied to other systems as well, that is, not specifically to the particular system that is being evaluated.

Depending on the type of information achieved through the evaluation process, it is common to talk about qualitative and quantitative evaluation, and accordingly about qualitative and quantitative measures (cf. Bernsen and Dybkjær, 2000). Qualitative evaluation is a descriptive approach that aims at forming a conceptual model of the system: what the system does, why errors or misunderstandings occur, which parts of the system need to be altered, etc. On the other hand, quantitative evaluation is an analytic approach that tries to address evaluation by objective criteria and achieve quantifiable information about the properties of the system with respect to special metrics. Often, qualitative and quantitative evaluations are considered synonymous to the use of subjective or objective criteria in the evaluation: descriptions are subjective whereas quantified metrics are objective. The use of subjective criteria means that there are no "right" or "wrong" answers, and the results of the evaluation are tendencies and preferences rather than claims with strong predictive power. However, the distinction between subjective and objective criteria is vague, and in fact, the criteria seem to form a continuum from strongly opinion-based views to generally accepted facts. For instance, such quantifiable factors as system errors, task completion, and dialogue success always have an element of subjective consideration in them since the values are dependent on the individual evaluators who annotate the data. The objectiveness of the factors is thus relative to the interannotator agreement among the annotators, and should be measured as part of the validation of the evaluation.

The metrics in quantitative performance evaluation are concerned with the accuracy and complexity of the system or its components. For instance, Möller (2005a) lists 36 different objective

TABLE 6.2: A confusion table.		
	EXPECTED/ CORRECT = YES	**EXPECTED/ CORRECT = NO**
System decision = yes	a	b
System decision = no	c	d

metrics, and divides them into five categories related to dialogue and communication, meta-communication, cooperation, task, and speech input. In this section, we briefly go through some of the most common and useful metrics used in spoken dialogue system evaluations.

Algorithms are usually evaluated with respect to the time (on a particular hardware) and complexity (the number of rules and inference steps, the use of memory), or considering the range of acceptable input types and possible responses. The most common measures for the accuracy of an algorithm or a statistical model are recall, precision, and F measure, as well as percentage accuracy and percentage error. These measures are calculated from a confusion table, that is, by cross-tabulating system decisions with respect to the expected, or correct decisions as shown in Table 6.2. Given the values a (true positives), b (false positives), c (false negatives), and d (true negatives), representing the numbers of the elements in each set, the different evaluation measures can be defined as follows:

Recall is the ratio of the items that the system has correctly classified or recognized as being of a certain class to all the possible items in that class, that is, how much of the expected classification is retrieved:

$$Recall = a/(a + c)$$

Precision is the ratio of the items that the system has correctly classified or recognized as being of a certain class, to all those items that the system has classified as belonging to this class, that is, how much of the recognized classification is actually correct:

$$Precision = a/(a + b)$$

Often, there is a trade-off between recall and precision (especially in information retrieval applications), and their relationship can be more conveniently expressed with the help of the F-measure, the harmonic mean of precision and recall. Given an equal weighting of recall (R) and precision (P), F-measure is simplified in the form:

$$F\text{-measure} = 2PR/(R + P)$$

It is also common to calculate the percentage of accuracy and percentage of error:

$$\%\text{-accuracy} = (a + d)/(a + b + c + d)$$

$$\%\text{-error} = (b + c)/(a + b + c + d)$$

However, unlike accuracy and precision, percentage measures are not very sensitive to small numbers of a, b, and c, and thus they do not provide the best measures if the size d of the nontarget elements is large; it is possible to attain high accuracy results by selecting nothing (Manning and Schütze, 2002).

Statistical evaluation metrics are widely applied to dialogue strategy assessment in user simulations where comparison of different user models and estimation of how realistic the synthetic responses are play the main role in the development of automatic simulation techniques (Georgila et al., 2005; Schatzmann et al., 2007). A survey of the modeling and evaluation techniques is given by Schatzmann et al. (2006), who also note that precision and recall may not be appropriate performance metrics for simulated user models, since these measures penalize for unseen user responses. However, the actually generated utterance may still function as an acceptable response in the dialogue context, although it may not be the "correct" or expected response.

The standard evaluation measure in speech recognition is the word error rate (WER), which calculates the portion of inserted (I), deleted (D), and substituted (S) words in the recognized sentence relative to the total number of words in the target sentence:

$$\text{WER} = (I + D + S)/\text{total number of reference words} \times 100$$

In language modeling, the standard evaluation measure is perplexity, which refers to the complexity of the search path. High perplexity means that there are more alternatives to choose from at each choice point, so errors are more likely. The BLEU-score is analogous to WER and used in translation and segmentation tasks as the error metrics (Papineni et al., 2002). The BLEU-score compares the target and translated texts by aligning them and calculating the inserted, deleted, or substituted words as in WER. Both have been criticized for only taking into account word strings and ignoring the semantics of the words and also for dismissing the fact that the utterances may still be acceptable, although not exact copies of the target utterances.

When evaluating spoken dialogue systems, measures for more holistic language understanding are needed since the system may be able to understand the user's intention despite its poor verbal presentation. For instance, to distinguish meanings rather than words, semantically oriented concept accuracy error rate can be used; this metric treats two words as equal if they refer to the same entity (Boros et al., 1996). Sentence understanding error rate can also be useful; if the sentence is mapped on to the same representation as the reference sentence, it is understood correctly even though all the words do not need to be recognized (naturally, recognition of the meaning carrying words is important). In the evaluation of the MIT Communicator system, Glass et al. (2000) used the metrics query density and concept efficiency, which check how efficiently the user can introduce new concepts to the system and how accurately the system can understand user queries, respectively. Query density is calculated as a mean of the new concepts that the user produces in each turn, whereas concept efficiency is calculated as a mean of the average number of turns required by the system to understand a concept. However, the problem with these metrics is that they favor user-initiative systems that minimize the number of turns.

Typical measurements for spoken dialogue systems are related to the system's efficiency and effectiveness in performing the underlying task. Efficiency can be measured by the length of the dialogue (number of utterances and number of words), the time it takes to utter one utterance or perform a task in full, mean user and system response times, the number of help requests, barge-ins, and repair utterances, correction rate, timeouts, etc., whereas effectiveness measures deal with the number of completed tasks and subtasks as well as transaction success. The definition of transaction success used in the ARPA evaluations regards a transaction as successful if the user was able to solve his/her problem without being overwhelmed by unnecessary information from the system. In practice, this is operationalized by counting errors and calculating the rate of correction/repair turns. Error measurement, of course, depends on the definition of an error, but in task-oriented dialogue systems this can be linked to the system's ability to recognize the correct task parameters and to produce the correct type of response.

The system's usability can be evaluated by asking potential users to test the system in realistic or near-realistic situations, and then collecting data about the users' opinions, attitudes, and perceptions of the system. For this, questionnaires and personal interviews can be used, as well as observations of the user's behaviour while they use the system, that is, kind of eavesdropping. Although observations may give an objective view of the interaction as a whole and introduce aspects that the users were not aware of during their use of the system, they are also heavily based on the observer's own subjective interpretation of the situation, and may thus overlook some important aspects of the user's preferences and internal motivation in their use of the system. It is also possible to try to quantify the user's performance in an objective manner, for example, by comparing it with the assumed expert performance within the same time span, and calculating the user's interaction rate as:

$$S = (P \times C) / T$$

where P is the percentage of the task (or tasks if there is a series of tasks in the evaluation) that the user manages to complete, C is the percentage of what can be performed (the expert's performance), and T is the time the user takes to perform the task.

To system designers, subjective user evaluations may give more informative data of the system properties than the more objective measures, since they focus on the user's first-hand experience of the system's usability and usefulness for the task. The quality of a system is usually measured by questionnaires where the users are asked to rate several system performance- and usability-related statements on a certain rating scale. Recommendations for speech-based telephone services (ITU-T Rec. P.851) concern three different types of questionnaires:

1. Those that collect information on the user's background at the beginning of an experiment.
2. Those that collect information related to the user's interactions with the system.
3. Those that collect information about the user's overall impression of the system at the end of an experiment.

The different topics in each set of questionnaires need to be translated into precise questions or statements depending on the goal and metrics of the evaluation.

To elicit reliable and correct information from the users, the design of questionnaires requires special attention. The questions should be clear, concise, and concrete, and they should also be unambiguous with respect to what system property is being referred to. Quantitative data can be achieved by formulating closed-ended questions as multiple choice or ordering questions, that is, the users are requested to choose the best alternative or order the given alternatives in a preferred order, respectively. For example,

> *How would you characterize the speech recognizer?*
> *1, excellent; 2, good; 3, ok; 4, bad; 5, cannot say*

or

> *Rate the following statements so that the order shows what you consider the most important property of the system to what you consider the least important property of the system:*
> *1. Easy to use, 2. Nice design, 3. Quick responses, 4. Clear help*

The questionnaires are often formulated on a Likert scale, which consists of statements to which the subjects specify their level of agreement. Agreement is expressed on a 5- or 7-point scale ranging from complete agreement to complete disagreement, for example

> *Statement: "The system is easy to use."*
> *I strongly agree/slightly agree/am neutral/slightly disagree/strongly disagree with the statement.*

It is not recommended to ask open-ended questions such as "How did you find the speech recognizer?" or "What did you like in the system?" since their analysis requires further interpretation of the free text. However, such questions can elicit useful qualitative data by allowing the users to express their views in their own words, and can be generally used at the end of the questionnaire to catch those aspects that did not come up with the questions but may be useful for system development.

To develop valid, reliable, and sensitive measures of users' subjective experiences with spoken dialogue systems is not an easy task. Hone and Graham (2000) discuss questionnaire-based subjective evaluation techniques and suggest the SASSI (Subjective Assessment of Speech System Interfaces) approach, which captures the users' perceptions in declarative questions that can be grouped into six dimensions: System Response Accuracy, Likeability, Cognitive Demand, Annoyance, Habitability, and Speed. Some of these, such as Annoyance or Likeability, are rather general dimensions, and their connection to usability has been questioned. However, given that interactive systems may also aim at providing enjoyable interactions that engage the users (cf. Section 6.7 below), these dimensions may produce the necessary data for assessing the user's perception of the system's positive effect.

Other usability question patterns have also been introduced. For instance, Adelman and Riedel (1997) proposed a MAUA (Multi-Attribute Utility Assessment) approach where utility is decomposed into three categories or dimensions: effect on task performance, system usability, and system fit. These can be decomposed into different criteria, and then further into different attributes, which have equal weight in the calculation of a utility score. Concerning usability, different evaluation methods can be used (usability testing, logging activity use, activity analysis, profile examination). They identify usability testing and system logs as effective methods for evaluating a stable prototype.

In data annotation and analysis, it is usually important to measure the reliability of the coding so as to obtain an estimate of how well the annotation categories describe the "true" nature of the phenomenon under investigation or, to put it in the other way round, how well the coders agree on the characteristics of certain elements that are being studied. The percentage agreement, that is, percentage of how many times the coders agree on certain categories concerning all the available cases, usually gives somewhat distorted and high figures, because it does not take into account the fact that in some cases the coders may agree because of mere chance and not because they think in a similar manner. To measure this type of intercoder reliability, Carletta (1996) introduced Cohen's kappa statistic in dialogue annotation. The kappa statistic measures agreement beyond chance between the annotators and their annotations of the dialogues. It distinguishes between the observed agreement (A_{obs}), that is, the agreement that appears in the data, and the expected agreement (A_{ex}), that is, the agreement that would occur by chance between the annotators, and measures the agreement as follows:

$$K = (A_{obs} - A_{ex}) / (1 - A_{ex})$$

The kappa statistic has been criticized because it does not take the annotator's own interests and inclinations into account: a strong preference for one category increases the likelihood that the coders have agreed by chance and consequently, the kappa score decreases. In such cases, Krippendorff's alpha can be used, because it makes chance agreement independent of individual preferences (DiEugenio and Glass, 2004). Kappa has also been used to measure task complexity (see discussion in Section 6.4.1).

In general, the metrics are chosen to measure the impact of relevant system properties to the overall evaluation goals, and thus they approximate the functioning of the system itself. However, it is not always straightforward to assess the relative merits of the many competing measures. For instance, in statistical modeling it is often useful to try to optimize the metrics so as to obtain as accurate and precise data as possible. However, optimization of the metrics does not necessarily optimize the entire system performance, since the chosen measures may be too general, too few, or off the point concerning the whole system's performance. A simple example is one-sided improvement of the speech recognizer without a matching improvement in the system's dialogue management: the more accurate recognition does not necessarily help in increasing user satisfaction if the dialogue strategies remain inflexible.

In language technology, Budanitsky and Hirst (2004) compared several evaluation measures for determining semantic relatedness between word senses, and noted that the best assessment of the applicability of a measure to the task is simply given by humans. If the applicability of the semantic relatedness component was evaluated by embedding the component into an NLP (Natural Language Processing) application, the results seemed to be fair as well, but if the evaluation was performed via a stand-alone component, assessment of the metrics and its applicability to the task was unclear. They further pointed out that the setup for human evaluation can be flawed due to the user's bias toward certain alternatives, whereas the computational measures suffer from "ad hoc relations," which do not lend themselves to suitable quantifications in any meaningful manner. The reason for this seems to be that the semantic relatedness relations are constructed in the context of language use rather than in an objective manner for computational measurements. Analogous conclusions can be drawn in the context of spoken dialogue system evaluation, especially concerning the usability and usefulness of the system. The user's subjective judgments may give the most reliable assessment of the system's usability, although they greatly vary from person to person, and even within the same person at different times, whereas objective evaluations may abstract over some attributes that cannot be expressed quantitatively and thus require focussing on certain properties which may not have any meaningful interpretations in the usage context as such.

6.4   EVALUATION FRAMEWORKS

In addition to deciding on the evaluation goals and metrics, a reliable method is needed to guide the evaluation process: evaluation methodology gives guidelines for data collection and validation of the data, and determines what counts as the appropriate value(s) for a given measure and a given system, how to obtain the valid values, and how to interpret the measurements with respect to the goals. In many cases, the choice of metrics and the methodology are closely related: quantitative evaluation usually requires statistical methods in the analysis, whereas functional and usability studies often collect data through user interviews and questionnaires, some of which can be further analyzed using statistical tools and some of which are qualitative in nature and in need of human interpretation.

The measured values should also be objective and reliable, that is, not invented for the task in hand but possible to obtain in repeated measurements. It is also important to clarify the amount and representativeness of the data required for the evaluation: statistical significance makes sense only if the input is large enough a sample of the whole input space and the studied phenomena have a similar distribution in the sample as in the actual "world". If it is not possible to collect enough data, or we are simply interested in a single individual or a unique system, we can talk about case studies with some reservations about the generality of the results.

Möller (2009) lists the following requirements for the evaluation methodology so as to guarantee that the goals and metrics fulfill requirements for correct measurements:

1. Validity—the method should measure what it is intended to measure.
2. Reliability—the method should provide stable results across repeated applications of the same measurement.
3. Objectivity—the method should achieve interexperimenter agreement on the measurement results.
4. Sensitivity—the method should measure small variations of what is intended to be measured.
5. Robustness—the method should provide results independently from variables that are extraneous to the construct being measured.

In this section, we discuss two different evaluation frameworks that are intended to provide a general methodology for evaluation. These are the PARADISE (PARAdigm for Dialogue System Evaluation) framework (Section 6.4.1) and QoE (Quality of Experience) evaluation (Section 6.4.2).

6.4.1   The PARADISE Framework

The PARADISE framework (Walker et al., 1997, 1998, 2001; Litman and Pan, 2002) measures the system's performance with the help of features related to task success and task costs, and assumes the main objective of evaluation to be to maximize user satisfaction by maximizing task success while minimizing task costs, see Figure 6.1.

Cost is measured with the help of efficiency measures, such as time and the number of utterances, and of qualitative dialogue measures[1] such as utterance delay, number of corrections, and repair ratio. Based on the task and dialogue metrics, a performance function can be produced indicating the relative impact of the various interaction and task parameters on the system performance. The para-

---

[1]Unlike qualitative evaluation discussed in the beginning of Section 6.3, qualitative measures here produce quantitative information. They refer to the properties of dialogue interaction that specify how well the interaction worked, that is, they describe the *quality* of the interaction.

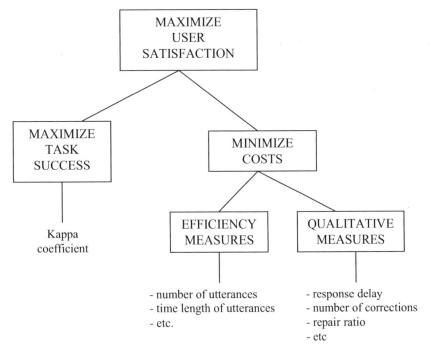

FIGURE 6.1: The PARADISE structure of objectives (following Walker et al., 1997).

meter weights are estimated by building a linear regression model, and an example of the performance function is given below, representing the application of the method to the TOOT data (from Litman et al., 1998):

$$\text{Performance} = 0.45N(\text{Comp}) + 0.35N(\text{MR}) - 0.42N(\text{BI})$$

where Comp denotes completed dialogues, MR is mean recognition, and BI is barge-ins. The function shows that the two significant measures for the performance prediction for this system are the number of completed dialogues and the speech recognition accuracy, whereas the number of barge-ins reduces the performance. The Completed measure is significant at $p < 0.0002$, Mean Recognition at $p < 0.003$, Barge-in at $p < 0.0004$, and altogether they account for 47% of the variance in User Satisfaction.

The performance function specifies the relative contributions of the evaluation parameters to the overall estimated user satisfaction, and thus it allows comparison of dialogue systems as long as the same metrics are used. Of course, if the systems do not exhibit the same interaction possibilities (e.g., if one of the systems does not allow barge-ins, or uses both speech and keypad input), a straightforward comparison of the systems is not possible: although the method itself can be applied to produce the individual performance functions, the performance functions themselves are not mutually comparable. This is because the novel functionalities in one system do not amount to parameters with zero weight in the other system's performance function—the new functionalities may have intrinsic dependencies on the system behaviour, and if the system is furnished with the new features, a new set of measures is also required. For instance, it can be expected that the possibility of barge-in increases user satisfaction because it would allow the user to cut off unnecessarily long system responses, but as shown in the example above, it also decreases the performance function. The solution then is to specify the parameters that characterize the new functionality and to clarify their effects on the system performance in more detail, for example, some barge-ins may indeed be signs of problematic interaction but some may be regarded as a welcome means of user control.

In PARADISE, the task is represented with the help of the attribute–value matrix (AVM) (see Tables 6.3 and 6.4), and the kappa statistic (see Section 6.3) is introduced as a measure of task complexity. The agreement between the information exchanged in the actual interactions (user answers) and in the ideal case (possible correct values) is calculated as the agreement between an annotator and an expert annotator, and the kappa value is interpreted as a measure of how hard it was for the user to perform the task with the system. The task success can thus be measured from the confusion matrix using the kappa statistic; high kappa values represent high agreement and high success rates.

The use of kappa normalizes the observed attribute values with respect to chance agreement, and it is claimed that this normalization provides a basis for comparing systems that perform different tasks. However, kappa is applicable only for information providing tasks that can be modeled with the help of an AVM where all the possible task parameters and their values are represented. Although the AVM representation provides an efficient and useful task representation, it is suitable only if the number of attributes and their values is small. If the numbers increase, confusion possibilities also increase and the calculation of agreement becomes more complicated. Also, the numbers on which to base estimations of the observed and estimated agreement become small, and

TABLE 6.3: An attribute–value matrix for a train timetable domain (following Walker et al., 1997).

ATTRIBUTE NAME	POSSIBLE ATTRIBUTE VALUES
DepartureCity (DC)	Milan, Rome, Torino, Trento
ArrivalCity (AC)	Milan, Rome, Torino, Trento
DepartureRange (DR)	Morning, evening
DepartureTime (DT)	6am, 8am, 6pm, 8pm

TABLE 6.4: An instantiated attribute–value matrix for a particular occurred dialogue (following Walker et al., 1997).

ATTRIBUTE NAME	ATTRIBUTE VALUE
DepartureCity	Milan
ArrivalCity	Rome
DepartureRange	evening
DepartureTime	8pm

large dialogue corpora are required in order to obtain reliable estimations for all the possible cases. Moreover, if the dialogues are concerned with open-ended goals such as planning, negotiation, or chatting, task complexity is related to the speaker's reasoning and varying knowledge of possible dialogue topics, and may not be possible to measure with a fixed AVM matrix at all.

The AVM matrix has also been adopted in statistical dialogue modeling to represent the task for learning dialogue strategies (Georgila et al., 2005) and for user simulations (Schatzmann et al., 2006). However, the flat AVM is also considered too simple to represent complex task structures, and for instance, Schatzmann et al. (2007) have replaced it with a representation called agenda (inspired by other agenda-based approaches), which captures a hierarchical structure of task goals in a stack structure, and also provides a dialogue history.

The main difficulty in applying the PARADISE framework to evaluation is the high cost for deriving the performance function. This requires elaborate data collection including the setting up of user tests and the annotation and analysis of the collected data. Although some of these tasks can be automated, a large dialogue corpus is needed, and it may be practically impossible to collect enough representative dialogues. As already noted, user simulations and automatic evaluation have thus gained interest as techniques that allow quick assessment of how well a particular system component works in practice.

Furthermore, linear superposition of interaction parameters seems too simplistic for such a complex task as HCI. Möller (2009) points out that although it is possible to remedy this by using nonlinear techniques, the correlations between user judgments and interaction parameters remain weak. This suggests that the metrics mix data from two complementary perspectives: the user's and the system developer's viewpoints. It is generally known that the user's and the system developer's conceptual models of the system can differ significantly, so it is crucial to distinguish the two viewpoints in the evaluation and select evaluation parameters and metrics, so as to allow the two perspectives to complement each other. Also, Hajdinjak and Mihelic (2006) emphasize the careful selection of regression parameters, and also the selection of an appropriate user satisfaction measure.

Moreover, they point out how normalization can affect the accuracy of predictions, and how speech recognition errors can influence the performance function.

Finally, it is not clear if the predictions can be traced back to the properties singled out by the performance function, or if they are dependent on the particular system. Walker et al. (2000) show that prediction is possible, although significantly reduced if the users of the system are changed from novices to experts. Möller (2005b) also observes that extrapolation from one system to another significantly reduces prediction power.

6.4.2 Quality of Experience Evaluation

Möller (2002, 2005a, 2009) offers another view of evaluation, the Quality of Experience (QoE), developed especially in the context of speech-based interaction systems. The framework emphasizes the user's experience in the evaluation process, and the overall goal of the QoE evaluation is to establish the level of system quality as perceived by the user. Although performance is regarded as the ability of the module to provide the function it has been designed for, quality indicates the value that the users assign to the system in regard to the task and service that the application is meant to deliver. Performance can be measured when corresponding indices exist, such as task success for effectiveness, elapsed time, or the number of user utterances for efficiency, and WER for speech recognition performance, but quality refers to system characteristics and the interaction flow as perceived by the users and can be measured through the evaluative judgments that the users form of the system quality by comparing what they perceive, that is, their actual experience of the system, with the expectations and knowledge they have of other similar systems.

In defining quality, Möller refers to Jekosch (2005), according to whom quality results from a perception and judgment process in which the perceiving subject (e.g., the user) establishes a relationship between the perceptive event and what he/she expects or desires from the service. Various factors such as the user's attitudes, emotions, experience with other systems, as well as knowledge of the task and the domain, influence the user's perception of the system and consequently, his/her judgments of the system quality. Quality can be subdivided into aspects such as effectiveness (the system provides the right functions), efficiency (effectiveness in relation to the resources expended), satisfaction of the user (experienced comfort, pleasantness), utility (involving cost measures), and acceptability (whether a potential user is willing to use the system). Some of these aspects can be linked to perceptual features and for a spoken dialogue system, important quality features deal with the system's intelligibility, sound quality, and noisiness, as well as with the user's perception of the system's understanding capability and flexibility of the system behaviour.

The QoE framework includes various quality aspects or categories of quality characterizing the quality perceived by the user: the speech input/output quality, dialogue cooperation, dialogue symmetry, communication efficiency, comfort, task efficiency, service efficiency, economical benefit, and utility. Some of them can be quantified with respect to performance measures. The quality aspects are influenced by different factors. For instance, agent, task, and environmental factors contribute to the overall usability and user satisfaction, whereas contextual factors influence service efficiency (cost, type of access, availability) and economic benefit. Altogether, they influence the system's utility and ultimately, its acceptability among the users.

One of the quality issues concerns the system's natural interaction—do the users perceive the system as easy and intuitive to use? (Cf. natural interaction and affordable interfaces as discussed above in Section 5.4.) It is likely that additional interaction parameters need to be extracted to accommodate the common cognitive mismatches between the user and the system designer, and that the parameters need to concern more detailed aspects of quality than what is currently used in efficiency, user satisfaction, and usability evaluation. Quality of interaction may be related to the system's perceived helpfulness, cooperation, and trustworthiness, which for their part are signaled by rather unnoticeable nonverbal cues such as the quality of voice, use of gaze and gestures, or the general communicative posture. The user's actual perceptions of the system are of course difficult to measure, and some objective measures of biodata and interaction structure should be combined with questionnaires, interviews and video analysis.

To assess the user's experience with the system, the user's previous expectations must be distinguished from his/her actual experience with the system. As noted, users have varying expectations of the system depending on their knowledge, attitudes, desires, and experience with similar systems, and the evaluation methodology should take these into account. An example of the expectation–experience measurement in evaluation is given by Jokinen and Hurtig (2006), who evaluated a multimodal navigation system. The impact of the user's expectations on the actual experience was measured using a two-stage evaluation process. The user is given the same set of evaluation questions twice: first, to collect the user's expectations of the system before the actual usage (after a short introduction to the system), and then, using the same questionnaire, to collect the user's experience with the system after the usage. The comparison between the answers is expected to reveal a more accurate view of the system properties than the ordinary one-stage evaluation, since the user's expectations are not specifically singled out in the post-usage assessment questionnaire alone. The difference between the experience and expectation scores shows how the user perceived the system: if the difference is positive, the experience fulfilled the user's expectations, whereas a negative score shows that the expectations were not met. The impact of the experience is estimated by the magnitude in the difference.

6.5   USABILITY EVALUATION

Often, usability evaluation is regarded as a task to be carried out in the final phase of the project's development life cycle. In the user-centred design framework, however, the user's needs and viewpoints constitute an important starting point, and usability considerations are an integral part of the development of the system, with new features and functionalities being iteratively introduced into the system. Some often-used techniques in usability evaluation include cognitive walkthroughs and heuristic evaluation (see overview of the different methods by Nielsen and Mack, 1994). We can also say that usability evaluation is performed by individual users with respect to their own personal needs, and by manufacturers of the system in the form of consumer reports where testing and comparison of the available products are presented.

The primary criteria in usability evaluation have been related to efficiency in task completion and the effectiveness of the different system properties. According to the ISO standards (ISO 9241), usability is calculated by adding up effectiveness (% of goal achieved), the system's efficiency (measured in terms of time to complete a task, the error rate, and the amount of effort), and user satisfaction (subjective rating scale). Also, factors linked to the users' expectations and the system's novelty features seem to affect the users' perception of the system. For instance, Jokinen and Hurtig (2006) noticed that users evaluated the same multimodal route navigation system differently depending on what they expected from the system, and the expected novelty features attracted more positive evaluations than those considered part of the state of the technology.

Issues related to affective and engaging design, and to enjoyable use of the system also seem important, besides the traditional paradigms where efficiency is the main goal. If the usage situation is relaxed in general, users are more likely to be tolerant of possible difficulties and problems in the system functioning. The user's emotional state affects their evaluations, and studies in experimental psychology have shown that the person's mood affects their behaviour, for example, sad participants produce more negative judgments about objects and people than do neutral or positive participants (Forgas, 1995). Recognizing the user's disappointment and acting upon it accordingly can be seen as facilitating positive evaluations as well as creating pleasant interaction situations. Much of current speech technology research thus concerns the recognition and analysis of the user's emotions and emotional speech, so as to anticipate potential problems and the user's frustration with bad dialogue interaction.

Social interaction also plays a role in pleasant and enjoyable interactions. Within Embodied Conversational Agent research, rapport and good feelings are found to be important aspects of communication fluency, and in the affective computing paradigm, the aim is to equip the system with the capability to recognize the user's affective and emotional state and react in a socially appropriate, empathetic way. For instance, recent work by Brave et al. (2005) demonstrated that an empathetic embodied agent was perceived as more likeable and trustworthy by the users than an agent that was not empathetic toward them (i.e., not showing friendly facial expressions or textual content). Bickmore and Picard (2005) argued in favor of relational agents, defined as computational artifacts that build and maintain a relationship with users over time, and use similar strategies that people employ in face-to-face conversations. The evaluation of their exercise advisor system showed that users readily engage in dialogue with a software agent, and that this also has a positive impact on the relationship that the users perceived between them and the agent.

Norman (1990) has summarized the new concept of design in the slogan "attractive things work better". According to him, human skills are ignored if the system design takes a machine-centered viewpoint where complex, precise actions are also required from the user. Cognitive artifacts can expand human knowledge, aid, and clarify our capabilities although, currently they often confuse and interfere rather than allow us to "overcome the limitations of brainpower". According to Norman the way to go is not toward entertaining applications, but to assist users to reflect the content from the user's point of view. A more human-centered design emphasizes less *experiential* (note: not experimental) ways of thinking; besides being "appropriate to the users' needs and the tasks they must perform", systems should also be compatible with the user's "fundamental capabilities" and people should find interfaces "comfortable." In the context of interactive systems, this type of experiential thinking can refer to systems that have been studied under the term "affective computing". In his later work, Norman (2002) talks about the emotional design of everyday things, and argues that people find things easier to use if they are not only functional but their design is also appealing to them.

6.6.   SPECIAL TOPICS IN EVALUATION

6.6.1   Semiautomatic Evaluation

As noted earlier, thorough user evaluation is labor-intensive, and usually it competes in time and resources with the development of new technology. Automatic evaluation of models and systems is thus useful in assisting and shortening the development process. Two related goals have been pursued when talking about user simulations and the automation of system evaluation: (1) to test certain models, techniques, and hypotheses by computer simulations, and (2) to replace the human user in the human–system interaction and evaluation loop by some type of user simulation. In this section, we shall discuss some of the work that aims to achieve these goals.

Computational modeling and simulation of some aspects of human behaviour have been studied from early on; besides supporting an accurate formulation of research hypotheses, simulation also allows testing of theoretical claims and proofs of the model's internal consistency without direct human involvement. For instance, Power (1979) modeled dialogue games between two software agents, and Carletta (1992) simulated some of the communicative posture choices that human agents can take in conversations by two computer agents that communicated and tried to minimize their total effort in communication. Pollack and Ringuette (1990) introduced the Tileworld simulation environment for exploring and benchmarking an autonomous agent's resource-bounded reasoning, whereas Walker (1996) introduced simulation to test different collaborative strategies produced by the theory of communicative autonomous agents. The benefits of the method concern both the precision and formalization of a theory, as well as the use of the results in the system design. Nowadays, however, computational modeling of human behaviour is used in cognitive studies and has largely moved from rule-based approaches to statistical modeling and evaluation.

Automatic simulation has also been regarded as a useful technique for rapid evaluation and development of dialogue systems when the setup for user studies is impractical or impossible. One of the early experiments with user simulations was conducted by Araki and Doshita (1997), who replaced a human user by a system that had characteristics similar to the system that was to be evaluated. A mediator introduced acoustic noise in the communication channel, simulating speech recognition errors, and interactions were then carried out between the two systems. Since then, automatic user simulations have attracted considerable interest. For instance, López-Cózar et al. (2003, 2006) and Torres et al. (2007) have used a rule-based user simulator to generate conversations to study the effect of confirmation strategies.

Recently, user simulations have also been introduced in the context of statistical dialogue modeling where optimization and evaluation of dialogue strategies have been the main objectives (Schatzmann et al., 2005a, 2005b; Georgila et al., 2005). In the statistical approach (see Section 2.4), dialogue strategies are learned from the corpora, but when comparing different strategy choices, a large amount of data are required since the variation of crucial choice points may emerge only after hundreds of dialogue interactions. To investigate the consequences of these choices, simulations provide a quick, and usually the only way, to collect enough data. The evaluation metrics for statistical user simulation are based on direct accuracy measures and indirect utility measures, and a survey of the different techniques and evaluation measures is given by Schatzmann et al. (2006).

One of the early undertakings in providing automatic evaluation and comparison of dialogue systems was the Japanese DiaLeague contest (Hasida et al., 1995). The evaluation of systems was carried out by making the systems "converse" with each other on subway routes, and the main goal was to provide an objective and synthetic method for evaluating the overall performance of dialogue systems. The systems' task was to find the shortest path in the context of its incomplete knowledge of subways routes and stations, and the dialogue was initiated in order to acquire the missing information from the partner. The systems used a specific interface language in communicating with each other so as to avoid problems with natural language processing. Each participating system obtained a score according to the number of completed dialogues it had with the other systems. The setup also allowed a human user to converse with the test systems, thus allowing human–machine data to be collected. The utterances were textual, but an interesting feature of the setup was that it used a web interface to allow the users to interact with the dialogue system at home and other suitable places besides the laboratory.[2]

The MeMo workbench (Möller et al., 2006) is a tool for automatic usability evaluations. It simulates the real users' erroneous behaviour, and relies on the conceptual errors or the "mental model errors" that users make when interacting with a system. The assumption is that quality and usability depend on the consistency between the user's mental model and the model foreseen by the system developer. The tool uses explicit task and interaction models for both the system and the user, and thus discrepancies between the user and the system models can be understood as errors in the dialogue flow. The user model is partially derived from the corresponding system task and interaction model, based on the observed behaviour of the user.

6.6.2   Standardization

The goal of standardization is to provide a reference framework and specifications for system development, so as to give equal footing for the building of practical systems. Standardization is mainly driven by industrial considerations, but it can also set the background and baseline for research purposes. Although standardization is not an evaluation framework, it can be seen as being formed on a general consensus of the best practices in system development, and recommendations support proactive activities in sharing experience and guidelines.

The work within ISO focuses on standardization and classification of materials, products, and services worldwide. It consists of several working groups that discuss relevant criteria, guidelines, and definitions for systems and services within their particular expertise area. Standards related to spoken dialogue system development are given in the technical specifications for Software engineering (Product Quality ISO/IEC TR 9126) and Ergonomic requirements for office work with visual display terminals (VDTs) (ISO 9241, Part 11: Guidance on usability, and Part 110: Dialogue principles). They try to ensure the suitability of systems and services for a given task, as well as their reliability, safety, and efficiency in normal use. The ISO standards also define usability—this is the extent to which a product can be used by specified users to achieve specified goals (ISO 9241).

Standards and technologies for Web-based applications are developed within the W3C group. The work includes specifications and tools that address dialogue and multimodal interaction properties especially in the web environment, and also provides quality assurance through a number of validators. As already mentioned, the W3C has also produced the VoiceXML markup language,

---

[2]The actual evaluations were conducted under laboratory situations, but of course, at the time of the Dialeague evaluations in the mid 1990s, web technology was rapidly developing, and provided interesting possibilities for ubiquitous interactions.

the promotion and extension of which are coordinated through the VoiceXML Forum, an industry organization for speech-based interfaces (see Section 2.3), and the working group for Multimodal Interaction is working on the W3C Multimodal Interaction Framework as the general architecture for multimodal systems as well as on the EMMA language as a data exchange format for the interface between input processors and interaction management systems (see Section 5.3).

For spoken dialogue systems research, standardization efforts provide a reference framework that supports evaluation and comparison of the systems and their properties against shared standards. Specifications also function as a technological language on which to build shared infrastructure and further research. Some tools (e.g., CSLU toolkit, RavenClaw/LetsGoLab toolkit), reference architectures (e.g., W3C MMI-architecture, DARPA Communicator architecture), and component technology (speech recognizers, speech synthesizers, parsers, information retrieval) already exist and are freely available. However, because of the explorative nature of research, it may be difficult, if not totally impossible, to agree on standards for research prototypes. An alternative to standardization is to share efforts aimed at constructing data, corpora, and other material that would enable further development of more advanced systems. This could be used as a starting point for empirical and experimental research on promising topics, as well as for sharing tools and systems that allow both teaching the existing state of technology and its further development. Although no general repository of dialogue related resources exists, some individual webpages provide useful links to systems, tools, and corpora (see Section 1.6).

In this context, it is also useful to mention linguistic annotation work that aims at establishing best practice guidelines and standards for language resources. The term *interoperativity* is used as a reference to the goal of supporting the creation and exploitation of (multilingual) language resources and enabling cross-lingual studies. It seems useful to adopt interoperativity as a design goal for dialogue systems, too, that is, to encourage collaboration across systems, tasks, and domains. The need for shared data and infrastructure is obvious when considering the evaluation of practical dialogue systems: their evaluation can be greatly facilitated through a shared starting point that would allow co-measuring of the criteria for improved performance and technologies. Also evaluation contests can be helpful in this respect, although it has also been pointed out that excessive focus on performance evaluation may lead to strategies where innovative approaches are traded off against getting a good score in the competition.

6.7   CHALLENGES FOR EVALUATING ADVANCED DIALOGUE SYSTEMS

More than 10 years ago, Hirschman and Thompson (1997) pointed out in their overview of the speech and NLP evaluation that there has been little focus on how users interact with a system. Nowadays, usability studies belong to the system development cycle, and HCI studies are part of the empirical basis for all system design. Although evaluation has become a crucial part in dialogue system development, and methods and metrics have developed considerably, there is still no generally accepted methodology of how to assess dialogue systems across tasks, applications, and users. In particular, there is a need for verifying specific evaluation questions and quantitative evaluation measures as indications of the system's particular characteristics that link to some general evaluation goals. Frameworks such as PARADISE and QoE (Section 6.4) provide a starting point for performance evaluation and user satisfaction, but they do not provide guidelines for preferred methods for data collection, parameter selection or weighing, choices which need to be determined empirically.

Concerning advanced multimodal and adaptive dialogue systems, the combined effect of the components on system performance and usability creates further challenges for evaluation since the system should be evaluated as a whole. Poor performance of one component may impact the overall performance, but it can also be compensated for by another component. The complexity of the task also affects evaluation; as discussed above, if the number of task parameters becomes huge, the AVM is not a suitable measure for task complexity but more complex structures are needed.

Multimodality adds a new dimension to evaluation through the evaluation of the various I/O modalities. Although it is clear that multimodal aspects make interaction richer and give more freedom to the users to select their preferred interface modality, a straightforward comparison of multimodal systems to nonmultimodal ones is too simplified a setup, and does not address such important questions as how exactly the different modalities contribute to task completion and user satisfaction, and what is the combined effect of the different modalities that provides extra value to the user compared with a similar unimodal application. The perceived naturalness is not so much due to the interaction with more modalities as such, but to the ability to use the multiple modalities for tasks and situations where they provide the best and most efficient means for interaction.

The use of each modality may be tied to the task (e.g., drawing or giving verbal instructions on route navigation), the context (privacy and politeness considerations may render speech in public environment unacceptable, so text and touch modalities are preferred), the user (familiarity with a modality, preferences, or physical capabilities determines selection of one modality over the others), and to other I/O options the user may have at his/her disposal: a modality can serve as a convenient back-off method if the preferred modality did not produce the desired output (e.g., using the touch screen if speech input did not work). Common evaluation techniques can be used to evaluate individual modality components such as the speech recognizer, speech synthesizer, handwriting pads, parsers, etc., but when the different modality components are used together, system performance needs to be quantified in a multidimensional way, and the evaluation metrics would need to capture the interdependence between modalities and tasks.

The relations between modalities, tasks, and user preferences could be represented in a PARADISE-type AVM, whereas kappa statistics could be used to capture variability among different users as well as within one single user when the single user uses the system in different situations. For instance, in the evaluation of the multimodal system SmartKom, the PROMISE framework

(Beringer et al., 2002) extended the PARADISE framework in this way to cover specific issues concerning multimodality. It abstracted over functionally similar modality technologies used in parallel (speech, gesture, and facial recognition), but weighted and related different modalities that work in cooperation or sequentially (e.g., gesture recognition is easier than speech recognition in a more limited domain). Usability questionnaires were adapted to the SmartKom scenarios (home, public, mobile), and included specific questions for the speech and graphical interface; the measures took into account the efficiency of each modality as well as the synchrony of the modalities.

Concerning adaptive dialogue systems, it seems like adaptive dialogue capabilities result in more successful dialogue systems. For instance, Chu-Carroll and Nickerson (2000) compared an adaptive dialogue system to two nonadaptive versions of the same system (one with a system initiative strategy and the other with a mixed-initiative dialogue strategy), and found that the adaptive system performed better than the others in terms of user satisfaction, dialogue efficiency (number of utterances), and dialogue quality (speech recognizer performance). On the other hand, evaluation of adaptive dialogue systems is difficult because of the complex issues that are involved in adaptation (see discussion in Section 5.2.). Höök (2000) has also pointed out that a comparison of an adaptive system to a nonadaptive one may not be possible at all; if adaptation is meant to be an inherent part of the system, the nonadaptive version is incomplete and thus not optimally designed for the task, so that a valid comparison is not possible in the first place.

Another challenge for evaluation is the spoken dialogue industry where the usability of commercial dialogue applications is of special importance. Here, systems should score high in performance and user satisfaction, that is, be usable. Recently it has also been emphasized that applications should have value to the users so as to be used by them. If the system brings some value to the users, they are willing to spend time and effort in learning the system functionalities and are also more committed to using it. The question of user satisfaction is thus related to the system's value for the user and to the user's willingness to use (and buy) the system in the future. Consequently, usability evaluation should aim at determining the effort the users are willing to spend on learning the system's functionalities, and whether they can learn to use the system in the amount of time available. In general, of course, the value may be difficult to measure since it can easily change depending on the situation and the user's needs and preferences, and even fairly modest applications can have a high value and be used frequently if they are of important help to the user.

Many usability studies also emphasize that the users do not only evaluate systems with respect to the objective task fulfillment, but they tend to value systems according to their personal likings, and appreciate an interface that is friendly and fun in addition to providing reliable and fast information. Although the focus in evaluation may remain on successful task completion and satisfying the user's requirements for efficient and reliable functioning, attention should also be paid to those aspects that deal with interaction fluency, smooth communication, and trust, that is, to those aspects that create rapport and good feelings in human-human communication. If the dialogue system aims at maintaining a certain level of social communication, the main concern is not necessarily efficient task completion but the ability to engage the user in the interaction. In fact, in applications that aim to act as companions or entertaining partners, efficiency may have quite the opposite effect: shorter dialogues are considered impolite and stressful, since it is the length of the interaction that contributes to affection and to the user's ultimate positive judgment. These types of meta-communicative goals are not related to what is accomplished, but rather to *how* something is accomplished using the dialogue, and consequently, the evaluation needs to focus on the means and strategies of interaction. It is obvious that these issues are especially relevant in spoken dialogue systems, which are integrated in robots and animated agents supporting more humanlike interactions, but it can be expected that new usability criteria in terms of enjoyable, affective, and engaging interfaces will also play a crucial role in the dialogue industry.

Evaluation of these new types of applications should take user engagement into account, and the user's experience of the system should be measured as part of the quality of the system. However, suitable metrics for measuring pleasantness and affectiveness of interactions are not yet available nor agreed upon. In interaction design, it has been argued that we need to change our language when talking about system evaluation, and instead of using the old usability-centred attributes of the system being efficient, effective, and satisfying, we should talk about the new type of applications that are addictive, cool, and delightful. The goal of the design should not only guarantee satisfactory task completion, but it should also bring a positive, pleasant experience of the use of the system to the user.

6.8   SUMMARY

This chapter has focused on the evaluation methodology and practices of spoken dialogue systems. It has provided an overview of the evaluation task and discussed different approaches, hypotheses, and types of evaluation. It has also presented various evaluation metrics, methods, and frameworks used in practical evaluation tasks. Finally, some challenges for evaluating multimodal and advanced dialogue systems were discussed.

As a conclusion, we can note that it seems difficult to propose a one-step general evaluation scheme, in which efficiency and user satisfaction measures would be obtained from a global set of parameters and which would provide reliable judgments about the multitude of aspects that concern the functionality, performance, usability, quality, and reusability of dialogue systems. For instance, Bernsen and Dybkjaer (2000) doubt whether it is possible to find a holistic idea that spoken dialogue systems evaluation research should even aim at, and which would eventually define what constitutes a good system and which type of system creates the most user satisfaction. Instead, a more practical way to proceed is to decompose evaluation into subtasks and cascade these sequentially so that several evaluation methods and techniques can be integrated into a composite scheme. The subtasks and their cascades may contain different goals and conditions, and thus require different types of evaluation, as well as different metrics that are appropriate to the specific goals. We can also add interoperativity that can support further development of dialogue systems evaluation and methodology, as well as assist in practical evaluation tasks by providing a shared starting point for the comparison of performance of new technology.

•   •   •   •

CHAPTER 7

Future Directions

The preceding chapters have presented an overview of spoken dialogue systems and have examined a range of different approaches and methods that are currently in use within the research community. Chapter 1 provided a general introduction to the topic of spoken dialogue technology, looking at the components of a spoken dialogue system, presenting some typical application types, and reviewing the issues of corpus collection and management, evaluation, and toolkits. Chapter 2 examined dialogue management in greater detail, while Chapter 3 reviewed various approaches to the handling of errors. Chapter 4 presented case studies of some systems that extend the basic dialogue mechanisms introduced in Chapter 2, while Chapter 5 discussed various dialogue phenomena, including cooperation, adaptation, and multimodality that need to be modeled if dialogue systems are to become more conversational and natural. Finally, Chapter 6 provided an extensive account of the issues involved in the evaluation of spoken dialogue systems.

Taken together, these chapters have illustrated how, within the past two decades, there have been significant advances in spoken dialogue technology. Looking to the future, it can be expected that spoken dialogue systems will become more usable and more widely used and accepted. However, there are still major challenges that need to be addressed and overcome. Currently, one of the major barriers to the wider deployment of interactive speech systems is the high speech recognition error rates that can occur, particularly when applications are used in noisy environments, or by speakers with unusual accents or speech patterns. Research in robust speech recognition is directed toward addressing these problems. However, given that speech recognition cannot be perfect, it is important to develop methods that compensate for poor recognition rates, such as the error handling techniques described in Chapter 3. Methods such as these should enable users to achieve their goals even when recognition is not perfect. The quality of speech output is also an important issue, particularly from the viewpoint of usability. Major advances have been made in text-to-speech technology with more naturally sounding voices becoming available in a wide range of languages. It can also be expected that with the maturing of the technology related to the advanced issues discussed in Chapter 5, the acceptability of spoken dialogue systems will also increase as the interaction would become more flexible and robust concerning the individual users' needs and expectations.

As spoken dialogue systems become more widely accepted, we can expect new types of application and new areas of deployment that go beyond the telephone-based systems for simple inquiries and transactions that are in common use nowadays. Multimodal applications combining speech with other modalities, as reviewed in Chapter 5, are an exciting and promising new development, particularly with the emergence of powerful handheld devices that combine the functions of mobile telephones with the computing power of PCs. There is a great opportunity for speech on these devices given the limitations of their size that make input and output using keyboard typing and large font presentation increasingly difficult. At the same time, there is likely to be a greater use of speech combined with other modalities in so-called ubiquitous environments and in smart homes. These issues are just beginning to be explored and will present major challenges for researchers in the next few years. Thus, we can expect to see a number of new research projects that address the issues of multimodality and of deployment in ubiquitous environments.

Enabling spoken dialogue systems to learn from experience is an important new research development, as reviewed in Chapter 2 and illustrated further in Chapter 4. Data-driven methods can be used to optimize dialogue management strategies and to overcome the issues arising from traditional handcrafted approaches. Although most of this work is still being carried out in research laboratories, it will be interesting to see to what extent these methods will eventually be applicable in commercially deployed applications.

7.1 CONVERSATIONAL DIALOGUE SYSTEMS

In this book, we focused predominantly on task-based dialogue systems, that is, systems that are designed to carry out a specific task, such as retrieving flight information, paying a bill, or troubleshooting a faulty piece of equipment. It is worth mentioning that another line of research, which has operated mainly in parallel with research on task-based dialogue, has been concerned with developing systems that can engage in conversations with users without necessarily performing any specific task. Rather than modeling human conversational performance with explicit models and experiments, these systems are based on the idea of simulating human conversation by giving an impression to the user of an intelligent "humanlike" dialogue partner. Indeed, there is an annual competition, known as the Loebner prize, in which conversational dialogue systems are judged according to the extent to which their performance is "humanlike" (http://www.loebner.net/Prizef/loebner-prize.html). These systems mainly use pattern-matching to scan the user's input for keywords and then output a response that matches the keywords from a set of responses in a database. In this manner, they appear to be engaging in conversation but there is no actual interpretation of the user's input or reasoning about the course of the conversation. With a sufficient collection of patterns and a method for avoiding repetitive responses by using randomly generated alternatives, such systems, also known as Chatterbots, can often produce a convincing performance in simulating conversation. ELIZA (Weizenbaum, 1966) and PARRY (Colby, 1975) are early examples of such systems, whereas Alice (http://www.alicebot.org/) is a current incarnation. The Loebner prize competitions have been held since 1991, and have been strongly criticized in that their goal is to fool the user into regarding the system as an intelligent agent, as well as for the fact that so far the systems have been based on text-based pattern-matching interactions. In 2009, the competition is for spoken dialogue systems.

Traditional spoken dialogue systems can be distinguished from conversational dialogue systems in terms of the technologies that they use to manage dialogue. However, these distinctions have recently become more blurred as dialogue systems have begun to use more data-driven methods for dialogue management using machine learning of dialogue behaviors, whereas conversational dialogue systems now use knowledge sources such as scripts to represent conversational topics. The European Union -funded COMPANIONS project (http://www.companions-project.org/), which aims to develop a virtual conversational companion for senior citizens, is an example of this convergence of technologies.

Research on natural interaction, embodied conversational agents, and robotics is also likely to make the distinctions vague. Not all spoken dialogue systems will be service-based information providers, and thus rich communicative capabilities, including ability to recognize and produce also non-verbal communication signals, are needed. One of the motivations of conversational systems is to elaborate the system's communicative competence, requiring understanding of human communicative skills. As pointed out by Cassell et al. (1999), truly conversational dialogue systems presuppose intuitive, robust, and functional interfaces, and if we implement as many human communicative skills as possible in the systems, they will become closer to "truly conversational" dialogue systems.

7.2   ACADEMIC AND COMMERCIAL APPROACHES TO SPOKEN DIALOGUE TECHNOLOGY

Research and development in spoken dialogue technology is carried out in academic as well as commercial laboratories. On the commercial front, there is a wide range of deployed commercial applications, whereas within academic circles there is a lively interest in the opportunities and challenges of this subarea of spoken language technologies. Although it might be expected that the results of academic research would carry over into commercial applications, this has generally not proven to be the case. Indeed, a gap has been identified between academic research on spoken dialogue systems and commercial work on the approaches that are being used to design, implement, and deploy interactive speech systems in commercially viable applications (Pieraccini and Huerta, 2005). Some attempts have been made recently to bring the two communities together and to attempt to bridge this gap, for example, in recent workshops addressing this issue (Weng et al., 2007a). However, at present there are two rather distinct communities interested in interactive speech systems, each with their own conferences and publications. One of the reasons for the distinction is that there are differences in emphasis between the interests of academia and those of the commercial world. Generally speaking, academic researchers focus on the following issues:

1. The technologies involved in spoken dialogue systems.
2. The use of technologies from artificial intelligence (AI), including more recently the use of statistical methods for various aspects of the dialogue management process.

The technologies involved in spoken dialogue systems—speech recognition, spoken language understanding, response generation, and text-to-speech synthesis—are also used in other spoken language applications. However, there are certain aspects that are particularly challenging for dialogue researchers. Speech recognition of conversational speech is particularly difficult because it involves continuous speech by a wide range of speakers. Moreover, conversational speech often includes disfluencies, such as hesitations and false starts, and is sometimes spoken in noisy environments, which makes the recognition more difficult. For this reason, some researchers in speech recognition focus on data from corpora of spoken dialogues. Similarly, spoken language understanding is more difficult due to the same disfluencies that cannot be easily captured using the grammars and parsers that have been developed for written texts, which are usually edited and thus more likely to be grammatical. For this reason, researchers in spoken language understanding have investigated more robust techniques for processing spoken language utterances and for extracting from them the information that is relevant to the application. Response generation for dialogue systems has to take account of how much information to present and how the information is best presented in a dialogue context given what has been previously said in the dialogue and the needs of the addressee, and considering aspects such as cognitive load, for example, when the user is engaged in another activity such as driving a car or when there is potential information overload. Finally, for text-to-speech synthesis an important consideration is the prosody of the output, including features such as phrasing and intonation, in order to produce speech that is natural and comprehensible for the user. Including prosodic features that convey different emotional states is a hot topic in current research.

Within dialogue management research, the emphasis until fairly recently was on the application of classical, rule-based AI techniques to give the system more "intelligence" and enable it to behave in a more humanlike manner. Within the past decade, however, the focus has moved away from traditional AI technologies toward the use of statistical methods and machine learning in dialogue management. Given that large corpora of dialogues are available, it is becoming more feasible to make use of these corpora for various tasks in dialogue research, such as automatic dialogue act recognition and labeling. Another rapidly growing research area, as discussed in Chapter 2, is the use of statistical methods and machine learning for dialogue management optimization.

Commercial developers, on the other hand, tend to focus on a different set of issues that can be grouped into the following:

1. Business needs
2. Performance factors

Regarding business needs, an important consideration is to explore business opportunities in terms of the types of applications for which a spoken dialogue system is useful. This includes assessing the benefits for users, providers, and suppliers, as well as ensuring return on investment. An important consideration is whether the new system will replace or complement a current system. A considerable amount of effort often goes into determining whether a spoken dialogue application will be successful on these grounds. Academic researchers do not have to concern themselves with these types of issues. On the other hand, issues related to the reliability of service and truthful information can be of both academic and business interest: relevant questions, as discussed in Chapter 6, concern the quality of service and the user's experience of the system. Moreover the creation of trust between the user and the application can be looked at from the point of view of providing usable and reliable service that the users are ready to pay for, or from the perspective of cooperative interaction that emerges from natural human–computer interfaces.

Regarding performance, it is important to ensure that the application is usable and will be accepted by users. For this reason, there is a lot of emphasis in commercial development on human factors issues and on overcoming or minimizing the effect of speech recognition errors. There are several books that include useful guidelines, based mainly on experience, on issues such as prompt design, choice of grammars, and call flow design (Balentine and Morgan, 2001; Cohen et al., 2004).

Of course, it is to be expected that the academic and commercial communities should have different agendas. At one extreme, academic researchers are motivated to make new contributions to engage in scientific exploration in order to "push back the frontiers of knowledge," whereas commercial developers are driven more by factors such as improving customer experience and generating revenue. The following are some ways in which academic and commercial interests could be brought together to work on projects of mutual interest.

The availability of dialogue corpora for training dialogue applications using machine learning is a major issue for academic researchers. Commercial dialogue applications generate large amounts of data involving real interactions between people and deployed dialogue systems. If some of these data could be made available to researchers, it would contribute immensely to research in new approaches to data-driven applications.

New technologies tend to originate in academic research, such as agent-based architectures or reinforcement learning-based dialogue management. Frequently, these new technologies are ignored outside the research laboratories and academic publications. It would be beneficial if there could be some intermediate stage between "pure" academic research and commercial deployment in which promising new technologies could be evaluated rigorously in terms of their potential for eventual commercial deployment.

On the other hand, it has been shown that users behave quite differently if they have a real need as opposed to laboratory situations (e.g., Ai et al., 2007). In evaluating dialogue systems, it is thus important to pay attention to the usability of the system, the user's need, and the usage situation in which the spoken dialogue system is intended to be used. By collecting usage information of the system in genuine usage situations when the system is available for the users but the situation is not controlled or coordinated by the researcher, it is possible to obtain valuable information about the system's usability and suitability to a particular task, and also to collect a huge amount of authentic data that are real human–computer interactions as opposed to WOZ dialogues where the computer part is played by the human wizard. Such authentic data are useful for data-driven approaches to dialogue management.

One of the issues besetting spoken dialogue technology is the lack of standards. VoiceXML has become a de facto standard for industry but it is usually viewed as lightweight and insufficient for academic research. Currently, efforts are underway within the VoiceXML Forum to investigate how VoiceXML could be extended so that it could be used in the development of more advanced dialogue systems. Academic researchers typically develop their own platforms and architectures that are appropriate for the particular theories that they are investigating. A greater use of shared resources would facilitate more useful comparisons between different research projects and would also contribute to the development of standard technologies. Already, a good deal of data can be shared (e.g., the dialogue data collected in the Switchboard and AMI projects) and many of the dialogue system frameworks are available under open software licenses. Although these types of resources are valuable, the problem often is the fact that the dialogue corpus is not collected exactly on the topic and domain that is of interest, or that the open source software is too large and complicated for a quick experimentation on a particular aspect of a dialogue system that the researcher would like to try. It is thus important to continue efforts for developing infrastructure, models, techniques, and resources that support flexible representation, robust reanalysis of data, seamless integration of different modules, as well as rapid experimentation and modeling of various interesting phenomena in interaction. Some of the more recent toolkits reviewed in Chapter 1 are beginning to address these issues.

7.3 CONCLUDING REMARKS

Spoken dialogue technology is an active and exciting topic that brings together researchers and practitioners from a wide range of backgrounds. The fact that there is considerable industrial interest in deploying dialogue systems adds to this momentum. There are many challenges ahead and we can expect many changes and advances in the technologies and methods used to develop and deploy future systems. This book has aimed to provide a comprehensive and readable introduction to the topic and to excite readers into becoming the next generation of dialogue systems researchers and developers.

References

Acomb, K., Bloom, J., Dayanidhi, K., Hunter, P., Krogh, P., Levin, E., and Pieraccini, R. (2007). Technical support dialog systems, issues, problems, and solutions. *HLT 2007 Workshop on Bridging the Gap, Academic and Industrial Research in Dialog Technology*, April 26, 2007, Rochester, NY.

Adelman, L., and Riedel, S. L. (1997). *Handbook for Evaluating Knowledge-Based systems. Conceptual Framework and Compendium of Methods*. Norwell, MA: Kluwer Academic Publishing.

Ai, H., Raux, A., Bohus, D., Eskenazi, M., and Litman, D. (2007). Comparing spoken dialog corpora collected with recruited subjects versus real users. *Proceedings of the 8th SIGDial Workshop on Discourse and Dialogue*, Antwerp, Belgium.

Alexandersson, J., Reithinger, N., and Maier, E. (1997). Insights into the dialogue processing of VERBMOBIL. *5th Conference on Applied Natural Language Processing*, 31 March–3 April, 1997, Washington Marriott Hotel, Washington, D.C., pp. 33–40.

Allen, J. F. (1995). *Natural Language Understanding*. Redwood City, CA: Benjamin Cummings.

Allen, J. F., Byron D. K., Dzikovska, M., Ferguson, G., Galescu, L., and Stent, A. (2001a). Towards conversational human–computer interaction. *AI Mag.* 22(4), pp. 27–38.

Allen, J. F., and Core, M. (1997). Draft of DAMSL: dialog act markup in several layers. The Multiparty Discourse Group. University of Rochester, Rochester, NY. http://www.cs.rochester.edu/research/cisd/resources/damsl/RevisedManual/.

Allen, J. F., Ferguson, G., and Stent, A. (2001b). An architecture for more realistic conversational systems. *Proceedings of the 6th International Conference on Intelligent User Interfaces (IUI-01)*, Santa Fe, NM.

Allen, J. F., Schubert, L. K., Ferguson, G., Heeman, P., Hwang, C. H., Kato, T., Light, M., Martin, N. G., Miller, B. W., Poesio, M., and Traum, D. R. (1995). The TRAINS Project: A case study in building a conversational planning agent. *J. Exp. Theor. AI* 7(1995), 7-48. Also available as TRAINS Technical Note 94-3 and Technical Report 532, Computer Science Dept., University of Rochester, September 1994.

Allwood, J. (1976). Linguistic communication as action and cooperation. *Gothenburg Monographs in Linguistics 2*. Department of Linguistics, University of Göteborg.

Allwood, J., Traum, D. R., and Jokinen K. (2001). Cooperation, dialogue and ethics. *Int. J. Hum. Comput. Stud.* 53, pp. 871–914.

André, E., and Pelachaud, C. (2009). Interacting with embodied conversational agents. In Jokinen, K., and Cheng, F. (eds.), *New trends in speech-based interactive systems.* New York: Springer.

Araki, M., and Doshita, S. (1997) Automatic evaluation environment for spoken dialogue systems. *Proceedings of the ECAI'96 Workshop*, Budapest. Lecture Notes in Artificial Intelligence 1236, pp. 183–194, Springer, Berlin.

Aust, H., Oerder, M., Seide, F., and Steinbiss, V. (1995). The Philips automatic train timetable information system. *Speech Commun.* 17, pp. 249–262.

Balentine, B., and Morgan, D. P. (2001). *How to Build a Speech Recognition Application—A Style Guide for Telephony Dialogues.* San Ramon, CA: EIG Press.

Bennewitz, M., Faber, F., Joho, D., and Behnke, S. (2007). Fritz—A humanoid communication robot. *Proceedings of the 16th IEEE International Symposium on Robot and Human Interactive Communication* (RO-MAN).

Beringer, N., Kartal, U., Louka, K., Schiel, F., and Türk, U. (2002). PROMISE: a procedure for multimodal interactive system evaluation. *Proceedings of the Workshop Multimodal Resources and Multimodal Systems Evaluation.* Las Palmas, Gran Canaria, Spain, pp. 77–80.

Bernsen, N. O., and Dybkjær, L. (1997). The DISC concerted action. *Proceedings, Speech and Language Technology (SALT) Club Workshop on Evaluation in Speech and Language Technology*, Sheffield, pp. 35–42.

Bernsen, N. O., and Dybkjær, L. (2000). A methodology for evaluating spoken language dialogue systems and their components. *Proceedings of the 2nd International Conference on Language Resources and Evaluation (LREC 2000)*, Athens.

Bernsen, N.O., and Dybkjær L. (2002). DISC dialogue engineering best practice guide to dialogue management. NISLab, University of Southern Denmark. http://www.disc2.dk/

Bernsen, N. O., Dybkjær, L., and Kiilerich, S. (2004). Evaluating conversation with Hans Christian Andersen. *Proceedings of the 4th International Conference on Language Resources and Evaluation (LREC 2004)*, Lisbon, 3, pp. 1011–1014.

Bickmore, T., and Picard, R. (2005). Establishing and maintaining long-term human–computer relationships. *ACM Trans. Comput.-Hum. Interact. (TOCHI)* 12, pp. 293–327.

Black, W. J., Bunt, H. C., Dols, F. J. H., Donzella, C., Ferrari, G., Haidan, R., Imlah, W. G., Jokinen, K., Lager, T., Lancel, J.- M., Nivre, J., Sabah, G., and Wachtel, T. (1991). A pragmatics-based language understanding system. PLUS Deliverable D1.2. *Proceedings of the ESPRIT Conference 1991.*

Black, L., McTear, M., Black, N., Harper, R., and Lemon, M. (2005). Evaluating the DI@L-log system on a cohort of elderly, diabetic patients: results from a preliminary study. *Proceedings of InterSpeech2005*, 4–8 September 2005, Lisbon, Portugal, pp. 821–824.

Bohus, D. (2007). Error awareness and recovery in conversational spoken language interfaces. PhD dissertation, Carnegie Mellon University, Pittsburgh, PA.

Bohus, D., Raux, A., Harris, T. K., Eskenazi, M., and Rudnicky, A. (2007). Olympus: an open-source framework for conversational spoken language interface research. *Bridging the Gap: Academic and Industrial Research in Dialog Technology workshop*. HLT/NAACL 2007.

Bohus, D., and Rudnicky, A. (2001). Modeling the cost of misunderstandings in the CMU Communicator dialog systems. *Proceedings of ASRU*, Madonna di Campiglio, Italy.

Bohus, D., and Rudnicky, A. (2003). RavenClaw: dialog management using hierarchical task decomposition and an expectation agenda. *Eurospeech 2003*, Geneva, Switzerland.

Bohus, D., and Rudnicky, A. (2008). Sorry, I didn't catch that! An investigation of non-understanding errors and recovery strategies. In Dybkjær, L., and Minker, W. (eds.), *Recent Trends in Discourse and Dialogue*. Springer-Verlag Series: Text, Speech and Language Technology, Vol. 39, pp. 123–156.

Bolt, R. A. (1980). Put-that-there: voice and gesture at the graphic interface. *Comput. Graphics* 14(3), pp. 262–270.

Boros, M., Eckert, W., Gallwitz, F., Gorz, G., Hanrieder, G., and Niemann, H. (1996). Towards understanding spontaneous speech: word accuracy vs. concept accuracy. *Proceedings of the ICSLP*. Philadelphia, PA.

Bos, J., Klein, E., Lemon, O., and Oka, T. (2003). DIPPER: description and formalisation of an information-state update dialogue system architecture. In *4th SIGdial Workshop on Discourse and Dialogue*, Sapporo, pp. 115–124.

Bouwman, A., Sturm, J., and Boves, L. (1999). Incorporating confidence measures in the Dutch train timetable information system developed in the ARISE project. *Proceedings of International Conference on Acoustics, Speech and Signal Processing (ICASSP)*, Phoenix, AZ, USA, pp. 493–496.

Brave, S., Nass, C., and Hutchinson, K. (2005). Computers that care: investigating the effects of orientation of emotion exhibited by an embodied computer agent. *Int. J. Hum.-Comput. Stud.* 62, pp. 161–178.

Budanitsky, A., and Hirst, G. (2004). Evaluating WordNet-based measures of lexical semantic relatedness. *Comput. Linguist.* 1(1), pp. 1–53.

Carletta, J. C. (1992). Risk taking and recovery in task-oriented dialogue. PhD thesis, University of Edinburgh.

Carletta, J. C. (1996). Assessing agreement on classification tasks: the kappa statistic. *Comput. Linguist.* 22(2), pp. 249–254.

Carletta, J. C., Isard, A., Isard, S., Kowtko, J., Doherty-Sneddon, G., and Anderson, A. (1996). HCRC dialogue structure coding manual. Tech. Rep. HCRC TR-82, Human Communication Research Centre, University of Edinburgh, Edinburgh, Scotland.

Carlson, R., Hirshberg, J., and Swerts, M. (2005). Special issue on error handling in spoken dialogue systems. *Speech Commun.* 45(3), pp. 207–209.

Cassell, J., Bickmore, T., Billinghurst, M., Campbell, L., Chang, K., Vilhjálmsson, H., Yan, H. (1999). Embodiment in Conversational Interfaces: Rea. CHI99, Pittsburgh, PA. http://citeseer.nj.nec.com/cassell99embodiment.html

Cassell, J., Sullivan, J., Prevost, S., and Churchill, E. (eds.) (2003). *Embodied Conversational Agents.* Cambridge, MA: MIT Press.

Cheyer, A., and Julia, L. (1995). Multimodal maps: an agent-based approach. *Proceedings of International Conference on Cooperative Multimodal Communication (CMC/95),* Eindhoven, the Netherlands.

Choumane, A., and Siroux, J. (2007). A model for multimodal representation and processing for reference resolution. *Proceedings of the 2007 Workshop on Multimodal interfaces in Semantic interaction (WMISI '07),* pp. 39–42.

Clark, H. H. (1996). *Using Language.* Cambridge, UK: Cambridge University Press.

Clark, H. H., and Wilkes-Gibbs, D. (1986). Referring as a collaborative process. *Cognition* 22, pp. 1–39.

Cohen, M., Giangola, J., and Balogh, J. (2004). *Voice User Interface Design.* Boston, MA: Addison-Wesley.

Cohen, P. R., and Levesque, H. (1990a). Persistence, intention, and commitment. In Cohen, P. R., Morgan, J., and Pollack, M. E. (eds.), *Intentions in Communication.* Cambridge, MA: MIT Press, pp. 33–69.

Cohen, P. R., and Levesque, H. (1990b). Rational interaction as the basis for communication. In Cohen, P. R., Morgan, J., and Pollack, M. E. (eds.), *Intentions in Communication.* Cambridge, MA: MIT Press, pp. 221–55.

Cohen, P. R., Morgan, J., and Pollack M. E. (eds.) (1990). *Intentions in Communication.* Cambridge, MA: MIT Press.

Colby, K. M. (1975). *Artificial Paranoia: A Computer Simulation of Paranoid Processes.* Toronto, Ontario: Pergamon Press.

Cole, R. A. (1999). Tools for research and education in speech science. *Proceedings of the International Conference of Phonetic Sciences,* August 1999, San Francisco, CA.

Cole R. A., Mariani, J., Uszkoreit, H., Varile, N., Zaenen, A., Zue, V., and Zampolli, A. (eds.) (1997). *Survey of the State of the Art in Human Language Technology.* Cambridge, UK: Cambridge University Press and Giardini. http://www.dfki.de/~hansu/HLT-Survey.pdf.

Constantinides, P., Hansma, S., Tchou, C., and Rudnicky, A. (1998). A schema based approach to dialog control. *Proceedings of 5th International Conference on Spoken Language Processing,* November 30–December 4, 1998, Sydney, Australia.

Danieli, M., and Gerbino, E. (1995). Metrics for evaluating dialogue strategies in a spoken language system. In: Empirical Methods in Discourse Interpretation and Generation. Papers from the *1995 AAAI Symposium*, Stanford, CA. Menlo Park, CA: AAAI Press, pp. 34–39.

Demberg, V., and Moore, J. (2006). Information presentation in spoken dialogue systems. *Proceedings of the 11th Conference of the European Chapter of the Association of Computational Linguistics (EACL-06)*, April 2006, Trento, Italy.

DiEugenio, B., and Glass, M. (2004). The kappa statistic: a second look. *Comput. Linguist.* 30(1), pp. 95–102.

Doran, C., Aberdeen, J., Damianos, L., and Hirschman, L. (2001). Comparing several aspects of human–computer and human–human dialogues. *Proceedings of 2nd SIGDial Workshop*, Aalborg, Denmark.

Dybkjær, L., and Minker, W. (eds.) (2008). *Recent Trends in Discourse and Dialogue*. Springer Verlag Series: Text, Speech and Language Technology, Vol. 39. Dordrecht, Netherlands: Springer.

Dybkjær, L., Bernsen, N. O., and Dybkjær, H. (1997). Designing co-operativity in spoken human–machine dialogues. In K. Varghese and S. Pfleger (eds.) *Human Comfort and Security of Information Systems. Advanced Interfaces for the Information Society*. Berlin, Germany: Springer Verlag, pp. 104–124.

Evermann, G., and Woodland, P. C. (2000). Large vocabulary decoding and confidence estimation using word posterior probabilities. *Proceedings of International Conference on Acoustics, Speech and Signal Processing (ICASSP)*, Istanbul, Turkey, pp. 2366–2369.

Fais, L. 1994. Conversation as collaboration: some syntactic evidence. *Speech Commun.* 15(3–4), pp. 231–242.

Forgas, J. A. (1995). The affect infusion model (AIM). *Psychol. Bull.* 119, pp. 23–47.

Fraser, N., and Gilbert, G. N. (1991). Simulating speech systems. *Comput. Speech Lang.* 5, pp. 81–99.

Georgila, K., Henderson, J., and Lemon, O. (2005). Learning user simulations for information state update dialogue systems. *Proceedings of the 9th European Conference on Speech Communication and Technology (INTERSPEECH–EUROSPEECH)*, Lisbon, Portugal.

Gibbon, D., Mertins, I., and Moore, R. (eds.) (2000). *Handbook of multimodal and spoken dialogue systems. Resources, Terminology, and Product Evaluation*. Boston, MA: Kluwer Academic Publishers.

Ginzburg, J. (1996). *Handbook of Contemporary Semantic Theory, Chapter Interrogatives: Questions, Facts, and Dialogue*. Oxford, UK: Blackwell Publishers Ltd.

Giorgino, T., Azzini, I., Rognoni, C., Quaglini, S., Stefanelli, M., Gretter, R., and Falavigna, F. (2005). Automated spoken dialog system for hypertensive patient home management. *Int. J. Med. Inf.* 74(2–4), pp. 159–167.

Glass, J., Polifroni, J., Seneff, S., and Zue, V. (2000). Data collection and performance evaluation of spoken dialogue systems: the MIT experience. *Proceedings of 6th International Conference on Spoken Language Processing (ICSLP)*, Beijing, China, 4, pp. 1–4.

Goddeau, D., Meng, H., Polifroni, J., Seneff, S., and Busayapongchai, S. (1996). A form-based dialogue manager for spoken language applications. *Proceedings of 4th International Conference on Spoken Language Processing (ICSLP'96)*, Pittsburgh, PA, pp. 701–704.

Godfrey, J., Holliman, E., and McDaniel, J. (1992). SWITCHBOARD: telephone speech corpus for research and development. *Proceedings of ICASSP'92*, San Francisco, pp. 517–520.

Goldberg, D., Nichols, D., Oki, B. M., and Terry, D. (1992). Using collaborative filtering to weave an information tapestry. *Commun. ACM* 35(12), pp. 51–60.

Gorin, A., Riccardi, G., and Wright, J. (1997). How may I help you? *Speech Commun.* 23, pp. 113–127.

Grice, H. P. (1975). Logic and conversation. In: Cole, P., and Morgan, J. (eds.), *Syntax and Semantics*, vol. 3. New York, NY: Academic Press, pp. 43–58.

Griol, D., Hurtado, L. F., Segarra, E., and Sanchis, E. (2006). Managing unseen situations in a Stochastic Dialog Model. *Proceedings of AAAI Workshop on Statistical and Empirical Approaches for Spoken Dialogue Systems*, Boston, USA, pp. 25–30.

Grosz, B., and Sidner, C. L. (1990). Plans for discourse. In Cohen, P. R., Morgan, J., and Pollack, M. E. (eds.), *Intentions in Communication*. Boston, MA: MIT Press.

Gruenstein, A., McGraw, I., and Badr, I. (2008). The WAMI toolkit for developing, deploying, and evaluating web-accessible multimodal interfaces. *Proceedings of the International Conference on Multimodal Interfaces*, October 2008, Chania, Greece.

Gupta, N., Tur, G., Hakkani-Tur, D., Bangalore, S., Riccardi, G., and Gilbert, M. (2006). The AT&T spoken language understanding system. *IEEE Trans. Speech Audio Process.* 14(1), pp. 213–222.

Gustafson, J., Boye, J., Fredriksson, M., Johanneson, L., and Königsmann, J. (2005). Providing computer game characters with conversational abilities. *Proceedings of Intelligent Virtual Agent (IVA05)*, Kos, Greece.

Hajdinjak, M., and Mihelič, F. (2006). The PARADISE evaluation framework: issues and findings. *Comput. Linguist.* 32, 2, pp. 263–372.

Hanna, P., O'Neill, I., Wootton, C., and McTear, M. (2007). Promoting extension and reuse in a spoken dialog manager: an evaluation of the Queen's Communicator. *ACM Trans. Speech Lang. Process.* 4(3), article no. 7.

Hasida, K., Den, Y., Nagao, K., Kashioka, H., Sakai, K., and Shimazu, A. 1995. Dialogue: a proposal of a context for evaluating natural language dialogue systems. *Proceedings of the 1st Annual Meeting of the Japanese Natural Language Processing Society*, pp. 309–312 (in Japanese).

Hazen, T., Burianek, T., Polifroni, J., and Seneff, S. (2000). Integrating recognition confidence scoring with language understanding and dialogue modeling. *Proceedings of 6th International Conference on Spoken Language Processing (ICSLP)*, Beijing, China, pp. 1042–1045.

Heisterkamp, P., and McGlashan, S. (1996). Units of dialogue management: an example. *Proceedings of ICSLP'96*, pp. 200–203.

Henderson, J., Lemon, O., and Georgila, K. (2005). Hybrid reinforcement/supervised learning for dialogue policies from COMMUNICATOR data. *IJCAI Workshop on Knowledge and Reasoning in Practical Dialogue Systems*.

Hirschman, L., and Thompson, H. (1997). Overview of evaluation in speech and natural language processing. In Cole, R., Mariani, J., Uszkoreit, A., Zaenen, H., and Zue, V. (eds.) *Survey of the State of the Art in Human Language Technology*. Pisa: Cambridge University Press and Giardini Editori, pp. 409–414.

Hone, K. S., and Graham, R. (2000). Towards a tool for the subjective assessment of speech system interfaces (SASSI). *Nat. Lang. Eng.* 6(3/4), pp. 287–303.

Hurtig, T., and Jokinen, K. (2006). Modality fusion in a route navigation system. *Proceedings of the IUI 2006 Workshop on Effective Multimodal Dialogue Interfaces*, pp. 19–24.

Hurtado, L. F., Griol, D., Segarra, E., and Sanchis, E. (2006). A stochastic approach for dialog management based on neural networks. *Proceedings of the 9th International Conference on Spoken Language Processing (Interspeech/ICSLP)*, Pittsburgh (USA), pp. 49–52.

Höök, K. (2000). Steps to take before intelligent user interfaces become real. *J. Interact. Comput.* 12(4), 409–426.

Jacquemin, C., Mariani, J., and Paroubek, P. (eds.) (2000). *Using Evaluation within HLT Programs: Results and Trends. Proceedings of the CLASS Pre-Conference Workshop to LREC 2000*, Athens. http://www.class-tech.org/publications.

Jameson, A., and Schwarzkopf, E. (2002). Pros and cons of controllability: an empirical study. *Lect. Notes Comput. Sci.* 2347, pp. 193–202.

Jekosch, U. (2005). *Voice and Speech Quality Perception. Assessment and Evaluation*. Berlin: Springer.

Johansson, S. (1995). The approach of the text encoding initiative to the encoding of spoken discourse. In Leech, G., Myers, G., and Thomas, J. (eds.), *Spoken English on Computer*. Harlow: Longman, pp. 82–98.

Johnston, M. (1998). Unification-based multimodal parsing. *Proceedings of the 36th Annual Meeting on Association for Computational Linguistics*, Montreal, Canada, pp. 624–630.

Jokinen, K. (1996). Cooperative response planning in CDM. *Proceedings of the 11th Twente Workshop on Language Technology (TWLT 11): Dialogue Management in Natural Language Systems*, Universiteit Twente, Enschede, the Netherlands, pp. 159–168.

Jokinen, K. (2006). Adaptation and user expertise modelling in AthosMail. *J. Universal Access Inf.*

Soc. Special issue entitled "User-Centred Interaction Paradigms for Universal Access in the Information Society." Feb. 2006, pp. 1–19. SpringerLink Online.

Jokinen, K. (2009). *Constructive Dialogue Management—Speech Interaction and Rational Agents.* Chichester, UK: John Wiley & Sons.

Jokinen, K., and Gambäck, B. (2004). DUMAS—adaptation and robust information processing for mobile speech interfaces. *Proceedings of the 1st Baltic Conference "Human Language Technologies—the Baltic Perspective,"* Riga, Latvia, pp. 115–120.

Jokinen, K., and Hurtig, T. (2006). User expectations and real experience on a multimodal interactive system. *Proceedings of the 9th Int. Conf. on Spoken Language Processing* (Interspeech 2006—ICSLP).

Jokinen, K., and Kanto, K. (2004). User expertise modelling and adaptivity in a speech-based e-mail System. *Proceedings of ACL 2004*, Barcelona, Spain.

Jokinen, K., Kerminen, A., Kaipainen, M., Jauhiainen, T., Wilcock, G., Turunen, M., Hakulinen, J., Kuusisto, J., and Lagus, K. (2002). Adaptive dialogue systems—interaction with interact. *Proceedings of the 3rd SIGdial Workshop on Discourse and Dialogue*, Philadelphia, pp. 64–73.

Jokinen, K., and Wilcock, G. (2001). Design of a generator component for a spoken dialogue system. *Proceedings of the Natural Language Pacific Rim Conference 2001 (NLPRS-01),* Tokyo, Japan, pp. 545–550.

Jokinen, K., and Wilcock, G. (2003). Adaptivity and response generation in a spoken dialogue system. In van Kuppevelt, J., and Smith, R.W. (eds.) *Current and New Directions in Discourse and Dialogue.* Dordrecht, the Netherlands: Kluwer Academic Publishers, pp. 213–234.

Jurafsky, D., and Martin, J. (2008). *Speech and Language Processing: An Introduction to Natural Language Processing, Computational Linguistics, and Speech Recognition.* New York: Prentice Hall.

Jurafsky, D., Shriberg, E., and Biasea, D. (1997). Switchboard SWBD-DAMSL, shallow-discourse-function annotation; Coders Manual. Tech. Rep. 97-02. University of Colorado Institute of Cognitive Science. Draft 13.

Kaasinen, E. (2005). User acceptance of location-aware mobile guides based on seven field studies. Journal of Behaviour & Information Technology, 24(1), pp. 37-99. Taylor & Francis.

Kerminen, A., and Jokinen, K. (2003). Distributed dialogue management in a blackboard architecture. *Proceedings of the EACL Workshop Dialogue Systems: Interaction, Adaptation and Styles of Management*, Budapest, Hungary, pp. 55–66.

King et al. (1996). Evaluation of Natural Language Processing Systems—EAGLES Final Report, EAG-WEG-PR.2, October 1996. Available at: http://www.ilc.pi.cnr.it/EAGLES/home .html.

Kobsa, A., and Wahlster, W. (1989) (eds.). *User Modeling in Dialogue Systems.* Berlin, Germany: Springer-Verlag.

Komatani, K., and Kawahara, T. (2000). Flexible mixed-initiative dialogue management using concept-level confidence measures of speech recognizer output. *Proceedings of 18th International Conference on Computational Linguistics (COLING)*, Saarbrucken, Germany, pp. 467–473.

Krahmer, E., Swerts, M., Theune, M., and Weegels, M. (1999). Problem spotting in human–machine interaction. *Proceedings of Eurospeech '99*, vol. 3, pp. 1423–1426. Budapest, Hungary.

Krahmer, E., Swerts, M., Theune, M., and Weegels, M. (2001). Error detection in spoken human–machine interaction. *Int. J. Speech Technol.* 4(1), pp. 19–29.

Krahmer, E., Swerts, M., Theune, M., and Weegels, M. (2002). The dual of denial: two uses of disconfirmations in dialogue and their prosodic correlates. *Speech Commun.* 36(1), pp. 133–145.

Kruijff, G-J., Zender, H., Hanheide, M., and Wrede, B. (eds.) (2008). *Proceedings of the ICRA 2008 Workshop: Social Interaction with Intelligent Indoor Robots (SI3R-2008), The IEEE International Conference on Robotics and Automation*, Pasadena, CA.

Larsson, S., and Traum, D. R. (2000). Information state and dialogue management in the TRINDI Dialogue Move Engine Toolkit. *Nat. Lang. Eng.* 6(3–4), pp. 323–340.

Lemon, O., Liu, X., Shapiro, D., and Tollander, C. (2006). Hierarchical reinforcement learning of dialogue policies in a development environment for dialogue systems: REALL-DUDE. *Proceedings of Brandial, the 10th SemDial Workshop on the Semantics and Pragmatics of Dialogue*, (Demonstration systems), 2006.

Lemon, O., and Gruenstein, A. (2004). Multithreaded context for robust conversational interfaces: context-sensitive speech recognition and interpretation of corrective fragments. *ACM Trans. Comput.-Hum. Interact. (ACM TOCHI)* 11(3), pp. 241–267.

Lemon, O., and Pietquin, O. (2007). Machine learning for spoken dialogue systems. *Proceedings of Interspeech2007*, Antwerp, Belgium.

Levin, E., Pieraccini, R., and Eckert, W. (2000). A stochastic model of human–machine interaction for learning dialog strategies. *IEEE Trans. Speech Audio Process.* 8(1), pp. 11–23.

Levin, E., and Levin, A. (2006). Evaluation of spoken dialogue technology for real-time health data collection. *J. Med. Internet Res.* 8(4), e30.

Litman, D., and Forbes-Riley, K. (2005). Speech recognition performance and learning in spoken dialogue tutoring. *Proceedings of INTERSPEECH-2005*, 4–8 September 2005, Lisbon, Portugal, pp. 161–164.

Litman, D. J., Hirschberg, J., and Swerts, M. (2000). Predicting automatic speech recognition performance using prosodic cues. *Proceedings of 1st Meeting of the North American Chapter of the Association for Computational Linguistics (NAACL)*, Seattle, WA, pp. 218–225.

Litman, D., Pan, S., and Walker, M. (1998). Evaluating response strategies in a Web-based spoken dialogue agent. *Proceedings of ACL/COLING*, pp. 780–786.

Litman, D. J., and Pan, S. (2002). Designing and evaluating an adaptive spoken dialogue system. *User Model. User-Adapted Interact.* 12, pp. 111–137.

Litman, D. J., Walker, M. A., and Kearns, M. S. (1999). Automatic detection of poor speech recognition at the dialogue level. *Proceedings 37th Annual Meeting of the Association for Computational Linguistics (ACL)*, University of Maryland, College Park, MD, pp. 218–225.

Lochaum, K. E. 1994. Using collaborative plans to model the intentional structure of discourse. Tech. Report TR-25-94, Harvard University, Center for Research in Computing Technology.

López-Cózar, R., de la Torre, A., Segura, J., and Rubio, A. (2003). Assessment of dialogue systems by means of a new simulation technique. *Speech Commun.* 40, pp. 387–407.

López-Cózar, R., Callejas, Z., and McTear, M. (2006). Testing the performance of spoken dialogue systems by means of an artificially simulated user. *Artif. Intell. Rev.* 26, 4, pp. 291–323.

López-Cózar, R., and Callejas, Z. (2008). ASR post-correction for spoken dialogue systems based on semantic, syntactic, lexical and contextual information. *Speech Commun.* 50, 8–9, pp. 745–766.

Manning, C., and H. Schütze (2002). *Foundations of Statistical Natural Language Processing.* Cambridge, MA: MIT Press.

Martin, D., Cheyer, A., and Moran, D. (1998). Building distributed software systems with the Open Agent Architecture. *Proceedings of the 3rd International Conference on the Practical Application of Intelligent Agents and Multi-Agent Technology.* Blackpool, UK: The Practical Application Company, Ltd.

Martin, J.-C. (1997). Towards 'intelligent' cooperation between modalities: the example of multimodal interaction with a map. In *Proceedings of the IJCAI'97 Workshop on Intelligent Multimodal Systems.*

McTear, M. (2004). *Spoken Dialogue Technology: Toward the Conversational User Interface.* London, UK: Springer.

McTear, M., O'Neill, I., Hanna, P., and Liu, X. (2005). Handling errors and determining confirmation strategies—an object-based approach. *Speech Commun.* 45(3), pp. 249–269.

Mehta, M., and Corradini, A. (2006). Understanding spoken language of children interacting with an embodied conversational character. *Proceedings of the Combined Workshop on Language-Enabled Educational Technology and Development and Evaluation of Robust Spoken Dialogue Systems. 17th European Conference on Artificial Intelligence (ECAI'06)*, August 28–September 1, Rivadel Garda (Italy), pp. 51–58.

Montoro, G., Alamán, X., and Haya, P. (2004). A plug and play spoken dialogue interface for smart environments. *Proceedings of 5th International Conference on Computational Linguistics and Intelligent Text Processing (CICLing 2004)*, February 15–21, 2004, Seoul, Korea. Lecture Notes in Computer Science, Volume 2945/2004. Berlin: Springer.

Moore, J. D., and Swartout, W. R. (1989). A reactive approach to explanation. *Proceedings of the 11th International Joint Conference on Artificial Intelligence* (IJCAI), Detroit, MI, pp. 20–25.

Möller, S. (2002). A new taxonomy for the quality of telephone services based on spoken dialogue systems. In: K. Jokinen and S. McRoy (eds.), *Proceedings of the 3rd SIGdial Workshop on Discourse and Dialogue*, Philadelphia, PA, pp. 142–153.

Möller, S. (2005a). *Quality of Telephone-Based Spoken Dialogue Systems.* New York, NY: Springer.

Möller, S. (2005b). Towards generic quality prediction models for spoken dialogue systems—a case study. *Proceedings of 9th European Conference on Speech Communication and Technology (Interspeech 2005)*, Lisboa, pp. 2489–2492.

Möller, S. (2009). Evaluating speech-based interactive systems—assessment and evaluation of speech-based interactive systems. In: Fang, C., and Jokinen, K. (eds.), *New Trends in Speech-Based Interactive Systems*. Springer.

Möller, S., Englert, R., Engelbrecht, K., Hafner, V., Jameson, A., Oulasvirta, A., Raake, A., and Reithinger, N. (2006). MeMo: towards automatic usability evaluation of spoken dialogue services by user error simulations. *Proceedings of 9th International Conference on Spoken Language Processing (Interspeech 2006—ICSLP)*, pp. 1786–1789.

Nielsen, J., and Mack, R. (eds.) (1994). *Usability Inspection Methods.* New York, NY: John Wiley & Sons.

Nigay, L., and Coutaz, J. (1995). A generic platform for addressing the multimodal challenge. *Proceedings of ACM-CHI'95 Conference on Human Factors in Computing Systems.* New York, NY: ACM Press, pp. 98–105.

Norman, D. A. (1990). *The Design of Everyday Things.* New York, NY: Doubleday.

Norman, D. A. (2002). Emotion and design: attractive things work better. *Interact. Mag.* ix(4), pp. 36–42.

Oh, A. H., and Rudnicky, A. (2000). Stochastic language generation for spoken dialogue systems. *Proceedings of the ANLP/NAACL Workshop on Conversational Systems*, pp. 27–32.

O'Neill, I., Hanna, P., Liu, X., Greer, D., and McTear, M. (2005). Implementing advanced spoken dialogue management in Java. *Sci. Comput. Programming* 54, pp. 99–124.

Paek, T. (2007). Reinforcement learning for spoken dialogue systems: comparing strengths and weaknesses for practical deployment. In McTear, M. F., Jokinen, K., Larson, J., Lopez-Cozar, R., and Callejas, Z. (eds.), *Dialogue on Dialogues: Proceedings of the InterSpeech2006 Satellite Workshop*, September 2006, Pittsburgh, PA, pp. 23–27.

Paek, T., and Horvitz, E. (1999). An uncertainty, utility, and misunderstanding. *AAAI Fall Symposium on Psychological Models of Communication*, North Falmouth, MA, USA, pp. 85–92.

Paek, T., and Horvitz, E. (2000). Conversation as action under uncertainty. *Proceedings of 6th Conference on Uncertainty in Artificial Intelligence.* San Francisco, CA: Morgan Kaufmann Publishers, pp. 455–464.

Papineni, K., Roukos, S., Ward, T., and Zhu, W.-J. (2002). BLEU: a method for automatic evaluation of machine translation. *Proceedings of the 40th Annual Meeting of the Association for the Computational Linguistics (ACL)*, July 2002, Philadelphia, pp. 311–318.

Paris, C. (1988). Tailoring descriptions to a user's level of expertise. *J. Comput. Linguist.* 14(3), pp. 64–78.

Pellom, B., Ward, W., Hansen, J., Hacioglu, K., Zhang, J., Yu, X., and Pradhan, S. (2001). University of Colorado Dialog Systems for travel and navigation. *Human Language Technology Conference (HLT-2001)*, March 2001, San Diego, CA.

Pérez, G., Amores, G., and Manchón, P. (2006). A Multimodal Architecture for Home Control by Disabled Users. *Proceedings of IEEE/ACL Workshop on Spoken Language Technology (SLT)*, December 2006, Aruba.

Pickering, M., and Garrod, S. (2004). Towards a mechanistic psychology of dialogue. *Behav. Brain Sci.* 27, pp. 169–226.

Pieraccini, R., and Huerta, J. (2005). Where do we go from here? Research and Commercial spoken dialog systems. *Proceedings of 6th SIGdial Workshop on Dialogue and Discourse*, Lisbon, Portugal, 2–3 September, 2005: pp. 1–10.

Pollack, M., and Ringuette, M. (1990). Introducing the Tileworld: experimentally evaluating agent architectures. *Proceedings of the AAAI-90*, pp. 183–189.

Power, R. (1979). Organization of Purposeful Dialogue. Linguistics 17: 107–52.

Price P., Fisher, W. M., Bernstein, J., and Pallet, D. S. (1988). The DARPA 1000 word Resource Management database for continuous speech recognition. *IEEE Conference on Acoustics Speech and Signal Processing*.

Price, P. (1990). Evaluation of spoken language systems: the ATIS domain. *Proceedings of the DARPA Speech and Natural Language Workshop*, Hidden Valley PA, pp. 91–95.

Purver, M., Ratiu, F., and Cavedon, L. (2006). Robust interpretation in dialogue by combining confidence scores with contextual features. *Proceedings of Interspeech 2006*, 17–21 September 2006, Pittsburgh, PA, pp. 1–4.

Reeves, B., and Nass, C. (1996). *The Media Equation. How People Treat Computers, Television, and New Medial like Real People and Places*. Cambridge, MA: MIT Press.

Rich, C., Sidner, C. L., Lesh, N., Garland, A., Booth, S., and Chimani, M. (2005). DiamondHelp: a collaborative task guidance framework for complex devices. *Proceedings of the 20th AAAI Conference and the 17th Innovative Applications of Artificial Intelligence Conference*. Pittsburgh, PA: AAAI Press/ MIT Press, pp. 1700–1701.

Rieser, V., Kruijff-Korbayová, I., and Lemon, O. (2005). A corpus collection and annotation framework for learning multimodal clarification strategies. *Proceedings of the 6th SIGdial Workshop on Discourse and Dialogue*, 2005, Lisbon.

Ringger, E., and Allen, J. F. (1996). Error correction via a postprocessor for continuous speech recognition. *Proceedings of the IEEE International Conference on Acoustics, Speech, and Signal Processing*, Atlanta, GA, pp. 427–430.

Rudnicky, A., Thayer, E., Constantinides, P., Tchou, C., Shern, R., Lenzo, K., Xu, W., and Oh, A. (1999). Creating natural dialogs in the Carnegie Mellon Communicator system. *Proceedings of 6th International Conference on Speech Communication and Technology (Eurospeech99)*, Budapest, Hungary, pp. 1531–1534.

Rudnicky, A., C. Bennett, A. Black, A. Chotimongkol, K. Lenzo, A. Oh, and R. Singh (2000). Task and Domain Specific Modelling in the Carnegie Mellon Communicator system. In *Proceedings of ICSLP2000*, Beijing, China, vol. II, pp. 130–133.

Sadek, D., Bretier, P., and Panaget, F. (1997). ARTIMIS: natural dialogue meets rational agency. *Proceedings of IJCAI-97*, pp. 1030–1035.

Schatzmann, J., Stuttle, M. N., Weilhammer, K., and Young, S. (2005). Effects of the user model on the simulation-based reinforcement-learning of dialogue strategies. *IEEE ASRU workshop Automatic Speech Recognition and Understanding*.

Schatzmann, J., Weilhammer, K., Stuttle, M. N., and Young, S. (2006). A survey of statistical user simulation techniques for reinforcement-learning of dialogue management strategies. *Knowl. Eng. Rev.* 21(2), pp. 97–126.

Schatzmann, J., Thomson, B., Weilhammer, K., Ye, H., and Young, S. (2007). Agenda-based user simulation for bootstrapping a POMDP dialogue system. *Proceedings of the HLT/NAACL*, Rochester, NY.

Scheffler, K., and Young, S. (2002). Automatic learning of dialogue strategy using dialogue simulation and reinforcement learning. *Proceedings of the Second international Conference on Human Language Technology Research*, March 24–27, 2002, San Diego, CA. Human Language Technology Conference. San Francisco, CA: Morgan Kaufmann Publishers, pp. 12–19.

Seneff, S. (1992). TINA: a natural language system for spoken language applications. *Comput. Linguist.* 18, 1, pp. 61–86.

Seneff, S., Hurley, E., Lau, R., Pao, C., Schmid, P., and Zue, V. (1998). GALAXY-II: A reference architecture for conversational system development. *Proceedings of 5th International Conference on Spoken Language Processing*, November 30–December 4, 1998, Sydney, Australia.

Seneff, S., and Polifroni, J. (2000). Dialogue management in the Mercury flight reservation system. *Proceedings ANLP-NAACL 2000*, May 2000, Seattle, WA.

Shneiderman, B. (1998). *Designing the User Interface: Strategies for Effective Human–Computer Interaction*, 3rd edn. Reading, MA: Addison-Wesley Publishers.

Sidner, C., Boettner, C., and Rich, C. (2000). Building spoken language collaborative interface agents. *Proceedings of the ANLP-NAAC*, Seattle, WA.

Singh, S., Litman, D., Kearns, M., and Walker, M. (2002). Optimizing dialogue management with reinforcement learning: experiments with the NJFun system. *J. Artif. Intell. Res.* 16, pp. 105–133.

Skantze, G. (2005). Exploring human error recovery strategies: implications for spoken dialogue systems. *Speech Commun.* 45, pp. 325–341.

Skantze, G. (2007). Error handling in spoken dialogue systems—managing uncertainty, grounding and miscommunication. PhD thesis in Speech Communication, KTH, Stockholm, Sweden.

Skantze, G. (2008). Galatea: A discourse modeller supporting concept-level error handling in spoken dialogue systems. In Dybkjær, L., and Minker, W. (eds.), *Recent Trends in Discourse and Dialogue*. Springer Verlag: Series: Text, Speech and Language Technology, Vol. 39, pp. 157–190.

Smith, R. W. (1993). Effective spoken natural language dialog requires variable initiative behavior: an empirical study. *Proceedings of the AAAI Fall Symposium on Human–Computer Collaboration: Reconciling Theory, Synthesizing Practice.*

Stephanidis, C. (ed.) (2009). *The Universal Access Handbook.* Boca Raton, FL: CRC Press.

Stolcke, A., Ries, K., Coccaro, N., Shriberg, E., Bates, R., Jurafsky, D., Taylor, P., Martin, R., Van Ess Dykema, C., and Meteer, M. (2000). Dialogue act modeling for automatic tagging and recognition of conversational speech. *Comput. Linguist.* 26, 3, pp. 339–371.

Sturm, J., den Os, E., and Boves, L. (1999). Dialogue management in the Dutch ARISE train timetable information system. *Proceedings of 6th International Conference on Speech Communication and Technolology (EUROSPEECH)*, Budapest, Hungary, pp. 1419–1422.

Sutton, R., and Barto, A. (1998). *Reinforcement Learning: An Introduction.* Cambridge, MA: MIT Press.

Thomson, B., Schatzmann, J., Weilhammer, K., Ye, H., and Young, S. (2007). Training a real-world POMDP-based dialog system. In Weng, F., Wang, Y.-Y., Tur, G., and Hu, J. (eds.), *HLT 2007 Workshop on Bridging the Gap, Academic and Industrial Research in Dialog Technology*, April 26, 2007, Rochester, NY, pp. 9–16.

Torres, M. F., Hurtado, L. F., García, F., Sanchis, E., and Segarra, E. (2005). Error handling in a stochastic dialog system through confidence measures. *Speech Commun.* 45(3), pp. 211–229.

Torres, F., Sanchis, E., and Segarra, E. (2007). User simulation in a stochastic dialog system. *Comput. Speech Lang.* 22(3), 230–255.

Traum, D. R. (1996). Conversational agency: the TRAINS-93 dialogue manager. *Proceedings of the Eleventh Twente Workshop on Language Technology (TWLT 11): Dialogue Management in Natural Language Systems*, Universiteit Twente, Enschede, the Netherlands.

Traum, D. R. (1999). Computational models of grounding in collaborative systems. Working Notes of AAAI Fall Symposium on Psychological Models of Communication, North Falmouth, MA, USA, pp. 124–131.

Traum, D. R., and Allen, J. F. (1994). Discourse obligations in dialogue processing. *Proceedings of the 32nd Annual Meeting of the Association for Computational Linguistics (ACL-94)*, pp. 1–8.

Traum, D., Roque, A., Leuski, A., Georgiou, P., Gerten, J., Martinovski, B., Narayanan, S., Robinson, S., and Vaswani Hassan, A. (2007). A virtual human for tactical questioning. *Proceedings of the 8th SIGdial Workshop on Discourse and Dialogue*, Antwerp, Belgium, pp. 71–74.

Turunen, M., Salonen, E.-P., Hartikainen, M., Hakulinen, J., Black, W. J., Ramsay, A., Funk, A., Conroy, A., Thompson, P., Stairmand, M., Jokinen, K., Rissanen, J., Kanto, K., Kerminen, A., Gambäck, B., Cheadle, M., Olsson, F., and Sahlgren, M. (2004). AthosMail—a multilingual adaptive spoken dialogue system for e-mail domain. *Proceedings of the COLING Workshop Robust and Adaptive Information Processing for Mobile Speech Interfaces*, Geneva, Switzerland, pp. 78–86.

Turunen, M., Hakulinen, J., and Kainulainen, A. (2006). System architectures for speech-based and multimodal pervasive computing applications. *Proceedings of the 1st International Workshop on Requirements and Solutions for Pervasive Software Infrastructures*, 7 May 2006, Dublin, Ireland.

Wahlster, W. (ed.) (2006). *SmartKom: Foundations of Multimodal Dialogue Systems*. Berlin: Springer.

Walker, M. A. (1996). The effect of resource limits and task complexity on collaborative planning in dialogue. *Artif. Intell.* 85, pp. 181–243.

Walker, M. A. (2000). An application of reinforcement learning to dialogue strategy selection in a spoken dialogue system for email. *J. Artif. Intell. Res.* 12, pp. 387–416.

Walker, M., Aberdeen, J., Bol, J., Bratt, E., Garofolo, J., Hirschman, L., Le, A., Lee, S., Papineni, K., Pellom, B., Polifroni, J., Potamianos, A., Prabhu, P., Rudnicky, A., Seneff, S., Stallard, D., and Whittaker, S. (2001). DARPA communicator dialog travel planning systems: the June 2000 data collection. *Proceedings of Eurospeech 2001*, Aalborg, Denmark, pp. 1371–1374.

Walker, M. A., Langkilde, I., Wright, J., Gorin, A., and Litman, D. J. (2000a). Learning to predict problematic situations in a spoken dialogue system: experiments with How May I Help You? *Proceedings of 1st Meeting of the North American chapter of the Association for Computational Linguistics (NAACL)*, Seattle, WA, USA, pp. 210–217.

Walker, M., Langkilde-Geary, I., Wright Hastie, H., Wright, J., and Gorin, A. (2002). Automatically training a problematic dialogue predictor for the HMIHY spoken dialogue system. *J. Artif. Intell. Res.* 16, pp. 293–319.

Walker, M. A., Litman, D., Kamm, C., and Abella, A. (1997). Paradise: a framework for evaluating spoken dialogue agents. *Proceedings of the 35th Annual Meeting of the Association for Computational Linguistics*, pp. 271–280.

Walker, M., A., Litman, D. J., Kamm, C. A., and Abella, A. (1998). Evaluating spoken dialogue agents with PARADISE: two case studies. *Comput. Speech Lang.* 12, p. 3.

Walker, M. A., Wright, J., and Langkilde, I. (2000b). Using natural language processing and discourse features to identify understanding errors in a spoken dialogue system. *Proceedings of the 17th International Conference on Machine Learning*, Stanford University, USA, pp. 1111–1118.

Wang, Y. Y., Yu, D., Ju, Y. C., and Acero, A. (2008). An introduction to voice search. *IEEE Signal Process. Mag.* 25(3), pp. 29–37.

Ward, W., and Issar, S. (1994). Recent improvements in the CMU spoken language understanding system. *ARPA Human Language Technology Workshop*.

Weiser, M. (1991). The computer for the 21st century. *Sci. Am.* 265(3), pp. 94–104.

Weizenbaum, J. (1966). ELIZA—a computer program for the study of natural language communication between man and machine. *Commun. ACM* 9(1), pp. 36–35.

Weng, F., Wang, Y.-Y., Tur, G., and Hu, J. (2007a) (eds.). *HLT 2007 Workshop on "Bridging the Gap, Academic and Industrial Research in Dialog Technology,"* April 26, 2007, Rochester, NY.

Weng, F., Yan, B., Feng, Z., Ratiu, F., Raya, M., Lathrop, B., Lien, A., Varges, S., Mishra, R., Lin, F., Purver, M., Bratt, H., Meng, Y., Peters, S., Scheideck, T., Raghunathan, B., and Zhang, Z. (2007b). CHAT to your destination. In S. Keizer, H. Bunt, and T. Paek (eds.), *Proceedings of 8th SIGdial Workshop on Dialogue and Discourse*, 1–2 September, 2007, Antwerp, Belgium, pp. 79–86.

Wessel, F., Macherey, K., and Schluter, R. (1998). Using word probabilities as confidence measures. *Proceedings of International Conference on Acoustic, Speech, and Signal Processing (ICASSP)*, Seattle, WA, pp. 225–228.

Williams, J. D. (2007). Applying POMDPs to dialog systems in the troubleshooting domain. In Weng, F., Wang, Y.-Y., Tur, G., and Hu, J. (eds.), *HLT 2007 Workshop on Bridging the Gap, Academic and Industrial Research in Dialog Technology*, April 26, 2007, Rochester, NY, pp. 1–8.

Williams, J. D. (2008). The best of both worlds: unifying conventional dialog systems and POMDPs. *Proceedings of International Conference on Speech and Language Processing (ICSLP)*, Brisbane, Australia.

Williams, J. D., and Young, S. J. (2007a). Partially observable Markov decision processes for spoken dialog systems. *Comput. Speech Lang.* 21(2), pp. 231–422.

Williams, J. D., and Young, S. J. (2007b). Scaling POMDPs for spoken dialog management. *IEEE Trans. Audio, Speech, Lang. Process.* 15(7), pp. 2116–2129.

Young, S., Adda-Decker, M., Aubert, X., Dugast, C., Gauvain, J., Kershaw, D., Lamel, L., Leeuwen, D., Pye, D., Robinson, A., Steeneken, H., and Woodland, P. (1997). Multilingual Large vocabulary speech recognition: the European SQALE project. *Comput. Speech Lang.* 11, pp. 73–89.

Yankelovich, N. 1996. How do users know what to say? *Interactions* 3(6), pp. 32–43.

Author Biographies

Kristiina Jokinen is an adjunct professor at the University of Helsinki and University of Tampere, Finland, and a visiting professor of intelligent user interfaces at the University of Tartu, Estonia. She received her Ph.D. at the University of Manchester, UK, and worked for four years in Japan as a JSPS research fellow at the Nara Institute of Science and Technology and as an invited researcher at ATR (Advanced Telecommunications Research) Laboratories in Kyoto. In Finland, she has played a leading role in several academic and industrial research projects concerning natural language interactive systems, spoken dialogue management, and multimodality. Her current interests focus on human nonverbal communication, gestures, and facial expressions. Her book *Constructive Dialogue Management–Speech Interaction and Rational Agents* has recently been published by John Wiley & Sons. She is the secretary of SIGDial, the ACL/ISCA Special Interest Group for Discourse and Dialogue.

Michael McTear is a professor of knowledge engineering at the University of Ulster. His main research interest is spoken dialogue technology. He is the author of the widely used text book *Spoken Dialogue Technology: Toward the Conversational User Interface* (Springer-Verlag, 2004), has delivered keynote addresses and tutorials at many conferences and workshops, and has participated in a number of European and nationally funded projects. He is on the editorial board of the journal *Artificial Intelligence Review* and regularly reviews papers for several international journals and conferences. He is a member of the Scientific Advisory Group of SIGDial, the ACL/ISCA Special Interest Group for Discourse and Dialogue. Recent research includes the application of spoken dialogue research to health-care systems and extending the scope of spoken dialogue systems to ubiquitous environments.